The Advanced Pool Player's Handbook

By

James R. Lawson

Que House
California

Published by Que House (USA) PO Box 2009, Manteca, CA 95336-1209 U.S.A.

Copyright ©1993 by Que House (USA)
All rights reserved

Except as permitted under the Copyright Act of 1976, no part of this publication may be reproduced or transmitted in any form or by any means, or stored in any mechanical, computerized, or other type of information storage and retrieval system, without prior written permission of Que House, P. O. Box 2009 Manteca, CA 95336

Printed and bound in the United States of America
International Standard Book Number 0-945071-91-4

The Advanced Pool Player's Handbook

Library of Congress Catalog Card Number:. 93-87435

Library of Congress Cataloging-in-Publication Data

Lawson, James R., 1937-
    The Advanced Pool Player's Handbook / by James R. Lawson. 1st ed.
      p.   cm.
    Includes Index.
    ISBN 0-945071-9194 : $ 18.95
      1. Pool (Game)--Handbooks, manuals, etc.   I. Title
GV891.L39   1993
794.7'3--dc20   93-45461
                                                CIP

10 9 8 7 6 5 4 3 2

First edition.

Contents

How to Recognize A Hustler	1
Pool Etiquette	3
Dress Codes	19
Tournament Play	25
The Calcutta	31
General Rules Of Pocket Billiards	41
Eight Ball	43
Eight Ball Variations	51
Nine Ball Rules	53
Texas Express Nine Ball Rules	61
Duties of a referee	63
Selecting A Cue	67
Definitions of Nine ball terms	75
General Glossary	79
Hustlers Glossary	93
Cue Makers	95
Travel Services	103
Index	111

How To Recognize A Hustler

A hustler is a pool player who attempts to play below his skill level without his opponent recognizing it. By playing below his skill level the hustler is attempting to sucker an opponent into playing for money. During play a hustler can be recognized in several ways. First will be the obvious experience with a cue stick. It will be apparent in subtle ways that cannot be hidden. Then there will be the shots played by the hustler. Many shots made will appear to be slop shots if call shot is not a part of the game being played.

When playing for sizable sums a hustler will make shots and shot sequences that are not seen or attempted by the average player. When the hustler is playing look at how he pockets object balls. Do they enter the dead center of the pocket. Is the hustler shooting hard or easy. Does the hustler leave himself shots that are straight in or are they at a slight angle. (angle shots are generally considered better since they usually allow the shooter to obtain position for the next shot without any extra effort) An experienced hustler will tend to shoot hard on a table that is unfamiliar to him. By shooting hard the object balls will stay on line and drop in the pockets without the line of travel being affected by the strange table rolls. The experienced hustler will also tend to play the cue ball off the rails without using draw shots. Draw shots tend to throw a player's stoke off and cause misses.

Another indication of a hustler is the play of a half table game. Whenever a player is seldom shooting an object ball over one half table away on his second shot he is a better than average player. When a player is playing a half table game and consistently leaves his opponent playing kick shots or a full table shot for the incoming shot, the player is probably a hustler.

A hustler never makes a spectacular shot and always wins by one or two balls. Should a hustler make spectacular shot in front of his mark or other spectators, it will appear to be a slop shot to most amateur players.

The hustler will attempt to force his opponent to make stupid mistakes at the table by his leaves. He will reinforce this psychological warfare with a condescending attitude and body language while on the sidelines. As the mark digs deeper in his pocket for money to play the hustler, the hustler may subtly taunt the mark with exclamations of good luck and comments on the mark's bad rolls. Just remember an experienced hustler can jaw a ball in a pocket as easily as he can make a clean shot!

If during a match or series of games, the hustler's opponent wins several games, the mark is being set up to increase the bet. When the hustler has his mark at what he considers the mark's maximum betting level the hustler will frequently win two out of three or three out of four games. Basically he will let his mark win just enough games to keep him interested without making it obvious to the mark he isn't going to win any money. Frequently the hustler will lose several games, then will want to play for double the original bet. He might win several games then and ask the mark if he wants to play for double or nothing. at this point it doesn't take long for the bets to reach forty or fifty dollars a game, or more. At this rate a slick hustler can extract a mark's entire pay check in several hours.

If you want to go out looking for a hustler, to watch him in action, you would want to visit the pool rooms that sponsor tournaments, and those bars and taverns where pool leagues play. You will find the hustlers in a pool room around tournament time, and in the bars and taverns on the nights the pool leagues play. As a general rule they do not play league pool or in tournaments since that would mark them as skilled players. They believe they can make more money by conning the less skilled players in these events into playing for money than they can by playing in the event themselves.

Because of the problems hustlers create, most knowledgeable room owners who cater to a local crowd refuse to hold regional or national tournaments. A poolroom that develops a reputation with local players as a place where hustlers hang out is a pool room that has a limited life span. At the same time a money game that draws a crowd in the local pool room is costing the room owner money. Spectators of this game aren't paying for time on the tables. So the owner of a room that is serving a local crowd doesn't want money games biting into his profits.

Should you want a list of rooms that have national and regional tournaments *The Pool Player's Road Atlas* from Que House provide such a list in an appendix.

Throughout this section I have refereed to a hustler as being a he. That was done for lack of a good non generic term. There are many excellent women players today who can hustle an average player just as well as a fellow can. In fact it is often easier for a woman to hustle a man because it is a macho thing for men to win at any sports competition, especially when the competition is against a woman.

Pool Etiquette

The need for pool etiquette

Not long ago, I was playing in a pool tournament for seniors. When I eliminated one player who expected to win the tournament he refused to shake my hand. This incident, coupled with the lack of uniform rules from region to region governing the various games of pocket billiards indicate there is a need for a set of rules -- billiard etiquette if you will -- which will govern the conduct of all billiard players..

The problems that occur in attempts to describe and define appropriate billiard etiquette stem from the different environments -- the pool halls and billiard parlors; the bars, taverns, and bowling alleys; the home recreation and game rooms; the senior centers; and all the other locations where billiards are played. These problems are compounded by the circumstances surrounding each contest -- casual play, solo practice, competitive practice, instruction, team or league play, play for money (betting & gambling), semiprofessional tournament, or professional tournaments. Finally, the rules of etiquette used by players at various locations tend to be tempered by the skill level of the players, the location of play, and their knowledge of the standard rules of the game.

The problems created by improper conduct while playing billiards are the same regardless of where the game is played. Bad manners in a sport of personal competition are inexcusable. When they are exhibited by adults they are doubly worse. Adults are supposed to know better. The bad manners of adults set examples and precedents for the younger players.

With these diverse circumstances it is obvious that any uniform code of conduct must be applicable in each individual situation. At the same time it must be flexible enough to allow for the different circumstances in which individual contests occur. It must also cover personal conduct and the use of equipment.

Equipment use

The typical equipment used for pocket billiards and furnished at a location consists of a table, billiard balls, ball rack, cue sticks, cue chalk, mechanical bridge, and hand talc.

As a rule, a player may use cue chalk, hand talc, mechanical bridges, and cue sticks of their own choice or design, as long as the use of the equipment is not disruptive of normal playing conditions or damaging to house equipment.
A breach of etiquette in the use of equipment occurs when the equipment is misused or abused. A breach in the use of equipment can also occur when accessory items are used incorrectly.

Obvious abuses of equipment include:

- Use of a pool table or the table rails as an ash tray. Modern commercial tables have rounded table rails so any item placed on the rail will roll onto the floor.

- Use of a pool table or the table rails as a coaster for any type of drink or drink container. Never set a drink container of any kind on the rails or cloth of a pool table. Many room owners forbid food or beverages of any kind within five feet of a pool table.

- Banging or dropping balls on the table top, or lofting them as they are taken out of the pockets for racking. Each time a ball bounces on the table it weakens the cloth and changes the playing characteristics of the cloth. In some instances the weakened cloth will develop small holes that require premature replacement of the table felt.

- Failure to replace the ball rack on it's hook or in the storage compartment.

- Placing or throwing a ball rack on the floor where it can be stepped on and cause personal injury or be broken.

- Failure to replace a mechanical bride on it's hook(s) under the table or in it's storage rack.

- Leaning a cue stick against a wall where it can fall to the floor.

- Slamming a cue stick into a wall rack at the end of play or failing to place a house cue into the wall rack at the end of play.

- The use of excess hand talc that results in talc prints of any size being made or left on the table felt.

- The use of cue chalk, pea bottles, or other items on a table rail as a target for shooting.

- Marking the table felt in any manner as an aiming aid before making a shot.

- Making a masse or jump shot in those locations where the use of such shots is prohibited.

- Sitting on the table at any time.

- Laying on the table during a shot in such a way that the shooter does not have one foot on the floor when the shot is executed.

- Practicing masse shots or jump shots on any table without the permission of the room management.

Social behavior

We have all seen the poor sport who doesn't know how to lose gracefully. At he other end of the spectrum are the braggarts -- those players who tell the world how good they think they are by bragging about who they have played and won games from. Neither of these exhibitions of social behavior are appropriate for pool players.

The rules that govern social behavior for pocket billiard players are:

- Shake hands with your opponent before and after a game or match. If you don't know each other it is a nice gesture to give your name, ask your opponent's name, and wish him/her luck.

- Doing anything that will distract an opponent or break the opponent's concentration on the game or shot at hand is considered sharking. This includes talking to the opponent while he/she is shooting or preparing to shoot; yelling at anyone; having a conversation with a third party; whistling or making other noises that will distract the shooter; intentionally moving the chalk away from the shooter so he must reach for it; holding chalk in your hand so the shooter cannot or forgets to chalk his cue; speaking to the shooter at any time between shots; or standing in the shooter's line of sight and swinging your cue stick in any manner.

- Arguing with an opponent over rules of the game. The game rules should be verified before play begins. It is each player's obligation to know the games' rules! This includes any house rules that preempt the official rules of the game. This is especially important in bar play where rules can be peculiar to that location.

- Attempting to break an opponent's shooting rhythm by delaying a game or taking an excessive amount of time between shots.

- Leaning or sitting on the table while your opponent shoots.

- Failing to control your temper and language during play and/or after play.

- Complaining about an opponent's good luck and your bad luck.

Unsanctioned Competition

Unsanctioned competitions are the most enjoyable and most dangerous aspects of pool. It can be the most enjoyable because the competition can be friendly and sociable where you can meet new people and make new friends. It can be the most dangerous because unsanctioned competition can involve gambling -- whether it is playing for a beer or money exchanges hands directly, a breach of etiquette in this environment can lead to a whole bucket of hurts and misgivings.

While all of the rules of equipment use and social behavior discussed earlier apply here, there are still more rules that apply in unsanctioned competition.

The most important rule of unsanctioned competition is:

- If you are not sure about what is happening, ask!

Application of this rule is immediately followed by the requirement that each player know, understand, and abide by the rules of the game being played.

This rule is especially important to you if you are playing an opponent who is unknown to you.

If you are competing with friends who in a location that has several tables, don't select the table next to the serious players who look like they are playing for money if another table is available. When approaching your table don't interfere with the shooters at the other tables. Remember the rules of social behavior: If you are unfamiliar with the placement and location of tables in the major pool rooms, the tables toward the front of the room tend to be used by the better players, with the table closest to the counter or cash register reserved for the better players.

- No walking in front of a shooter while he or she is shooting.
- No shouting at friends across the room.
- If you are a spectator, comments of any kind about a shooter, or talking to the shooter while he or she is shooting is considered a serious breach of etiquette.

One situation you can encounter in unsanctioned competitive play is someone wanting to borrow another player's personal cue stick. Unless an offer is made, to ask to use someone's personal cue is akin to asking to borrow money from a stranger. Loans of this kind are seldom made.

It should be noted here that a spectator is never allowed to call fouls or inform a player about an opponent's foul. Unless the session is instructional spectators are never allowed to coach or advise other players.

The breaches of etiquette that have been described up to this point are usually not intentional. They are the result of bad habits. Most amateur players are simply not aware of the importance of table manners in a bar or billiard parlor. The lack of these social graces can label the uneducated a social misfit at the pool table. In the wrong crowd the lack of table manners can even lead to serious injuries if the losing players feel they have been hustled.

The main thing you want to remember is that if you see money changing hands, the players are not engaged in casual play. Money may be actual cash or any type of coin placed under the rail at the various table diamonds, the use of the overhead scoring markers or beads, and the use of the game counters embedded in the foot rail of the table.

Cash settlement under these conditions usually occurs at the end of play. Very often settlement will be made outside the location, in the parking lot.

Coins on or under a rail of a coin operated bar table mean someone is waiting to play the winner of the game in progress. It is not an absolute sign that money is changing hands.

In the tavern environment, the stakes are frequently the cost of a bottle of beer. Since a good player can seldom drink all the beer he or she will win, the bartender usually issues a beer chit for each beer won. These chits are then exchanged at the end of play for cash. However, this method places the barkeep in the tenuous position of being a bookkeeper for the winner -- and the chit count can be in question at times. With this system there is little the winner can do if the count is in question except demand payment by chit at the conclusion of each game.

When you are playing for money, always find out who your opponent is, where he is from, and what your chances of winning are. And never, never, never bet more than you can afford to lose.

If you are playing for stakes over the cost of a bottle of beer, it is not unusual to require settlement after each game. If the stakes are such that there is a question that either or both players might not be able to cover the wager, the bets of both players should be placed in a neutral place.

It has been suggested by one writer about bar pool that a link of the table light chain is a reasonable depository for all bets. However, use of this location makes it obvious that you are betting on the game.

It can also allow an opportunist to grab the cash when the players are not looking.

Another suggestion that is made when the stakes are substantial, is to have a third party hold the stakes. The problem here is obvious. With a substantial stake in hand the third party may disappear. If the third party is unknown to you, you could end up having to contend with two individuals who are unwilling to surrender your winnings to you.

Having dealt with these possibilities, it is customary on time pay tables for the winner to pay for the table time.

In the same vein, it is not unusual for money players to concede balls on the table to an opponent he feels will run out anyway. This reduces the charges for table time.

On coin operated tables it is customary for the challenger to pay for the game and rack the balls. If several people are waiting to play on a table, a coin (usually a quarter) is generally placed on or under the foot rail or coin mechanism rail.

It is also customary to ask if the winner is playing for anything before inserting your quarter. A good many disputes arise when a challenger does not establish the stakes before play begins.

Disputes can also arise if any house rules are not mentioned before play begins. In all locations that are new to you it is best to ask about house rules before play begins.

Regardless of what level or type of competition you are engaged in, or the location where you are playing, you can obtain serious abrasions, contusions, and bruises if you deliberately interfere with, touch, or catch a ball as it enters a pocket. The knowledgeable player doesn't even want to appear as if he has interfered with pocketing a ball.

During casual play with friends when money is not involved it is considered appropriate to call fouls on yourself if you are aware of the committing the fowl -- even if your opponent did not see you commit the foul. (Double hit of the cue ball, touching another ball with your hand or cue stick, are common examples of how a foul can be committed without the opposition seeing it.) In competition where a game referee is present it is the referee's job and responsibility to observe and call all fouls.

There are situations that can cause problems during a game if the rules are not established before hand. For example, at what point in a game of Eight Ball is a ball considered in or out of the kitchen? Some individuals feel the entire ball must be out of the kitchen. Others believe that if the base of the ball, where it touches the table, is out of the kitchen that the entire ball can be considered out of the kitchen. The easy way to resolve this is to let your opposition determine whether the ball is in or out of the kitchen.

Another example is when it appears you may strike your opponent's object ball or the eight ball before striking your object ball. Shooting balls where this might occur frequently creates disputes between players. The best policy is to avoid shooting this type of shot at any cost -- if the game is unrefereed. If it is refereed the referee will make the decision on whether it was a legal shot.

Hustling and Sharking

Many uniformed spectators and players confuse the terms hustling and sharking. Hustling is the practice of adjusting the apparent skill of a player to match the skill level of a player of lessor skill. The hustler then manipulates the competition into making a bet on a game. At this time the hustler will frequently allow the lessor player to win several games and increase the amount wagered. When the stakes are high enough the hustler will begin to win on what appear to be lucky shots. As the session continues the hustler will continue to win the majority of the games, with the lesser player allowed to win a game occasionally to keep him playing.

Any time a player is playing below his skill level it is an attempt to hustle the competition. There have been cases where an ambidextrous right handed player would start play with his left (off) hand and offer a handicap to the opposition by playing with his other (right) hand.

With this description of the art of hustling it is obvious that hustlers are not welcome in any reputable location where pocket billiards are played. You will frequently find hustlers are road players and tend to play in and visit the locations where major tournaments and leagues play. A good start on where to find and observe hustlers in action would the locations listed in the appendices of this book.

Sharking is the deliberate distraction of a shooter. It is attempt to win by any non violent means available. Sharking is the use of any action that can break the shooting rhythm of an opponent. While it is normally associated with intentional distraction during play it also includes such things as making unusually long rest breaks.

General good manners:

Up to this point you have been introduced to all the negative aspects of the game and what not to do. There are some things you can do to add to your enjoyment of the game.

- **Coin operated tables:**

    When playing on a coin operated table it is customary for the winner of each game to play the next individual who has placed a coin under the rail. If there are no coins under the rail and the table appears to be free it is polite to ask if the table is free or "belongs" to someone -- the last winning player.

    It is generally considered to be impolite to place a coin on a table if a couple are playing on a coin operated table and they appear to be on a date.

    As the incoming player you are expected to rack the balls and the individual who won the last game will usually make the break. (Check on this though -- in some areas of the country the loser or incoming player has the break.)

If you are standing closest to the ball drop and scratch the cue ball it is considered polite to remove the ball and hand it to the competition.

It is considered polite to lay your cue across the table so the cue ball cannot be shot at the racked balls until the rack has been placed on it's hook or in it's slot.

It is considered very impolite to break the balls until the person racking them has stepped away from the table.

- **Time pay tables**

    With time pay tables you are in a different environment. Generally you are at a pool hall where the clientele has come to play pool. While all the rules associated with coin operated tables cannot apply, those for racking and scratch balls do.

    As the incoming player you are expected to rack the balls and the individual who won the last game will usually make the break. (Check on this though -- in some areas of the country the loser or incoming player has the break.)

    If you are standing closest to the ball drop and scratch the cue ball it is considered polite to remove the ball and hand it to the competition. (This is also true if you a playing on a table that does not have a ball drop and the balls remain in the pockets where they were shot.)

    It is considered polite to lay your cue across the table so the cue ball cannot be shot at the racked balls until the rack has been placed on it's hook or in it's slot.

It is considered very impolite to break the balls until the person racking them has stepped away from the table.

Sanctioned Competition

Sanctioned competition can involve all of the following:

- Amateur tournament play at the local billiard parlor, pool room, tavern, bar, or pub.

- League play of any type. (League play is defined as regularly scheduled matches between teams of two to five people who are sponsored by local businesses with at least six teams in the league.) Included in this category is the end of season tournaments sponsored by league operators.

- Pro-Am and professional tournaments.

As a rule, the organization sanctioning the event establishes the rules of conduct and play for each match. These rules are usually covered in a player's meeting (or the player's handbook for regular league play). For amateur players the dress codes are usually presented by the tournament director during a players meeting which is held an hour or so before the tournament begins or on the evening preceding the tournament. In the professional matches each player is usually requested to sign a statement prior to the match that he or she understand the rules ands will abide by them before he or she can play.

Regardless of who is running the competition or the type of sanctioned play, there are still universal rules of conduct that must be observed.

Since a competitive player is at all times an athlete, a performer, and a representative of the sport, the player is expected at all times to act and look like a lady or gentleman, as the case may be.

When committing to play in a tournament it is considered good manners to sign up early and pay the entry fee when signing up.

In any type of competitive play each player is expected to be on time and ready to play at the designated match time. In professional play failure to be on time could be construed as deliberate delay of the game, or unsportsmanlike conduct and lead to automatic forfeiture of the match.

It is always considered to be good manners to shake hands before any match with an opponent. It is even acceptable to wish an opponent luck or say "May the best player win."

In sanctioned play, it is each player's responsibility to inspect the equipment for flaws or problems before competitive play begins. After play has begun, the legality of the equipment in use cannot be challenged. This is especially true of the weight and size of cue balls used on coin operated tables. To complain about the equipment after play begins can be considered unsportsmanlike conduct.

During competition, the non shooting player is expected to stay seated at all times. This allows the shooter to concentrate soly on the game with minimal distractions.

Intentional distracting a shooter is considered unsportsmanlike conduct and can result in the perpetrator being disqualified from the competition.

In any type of sanctioned play, unless it is specifically written into the rules, it is considered unsportsmanlike conduct to coach another player at any time during play. Breach of this code of conduct can cost a player and/or a team a match. In the right circumstances it can get both the player and the coach ejected from a match.

In serious sanctioned events, each game has a tournament official who acts as a referee and rack person. This individual is in complete charge of the match where he or she is officiating. The referee will be responsive to player inquiries that require objective answers -- i.e., a player may ask if a ball is in the kitchen, if the table is open, etc. A referee can not provide a subjective opinion -- i.e., whether a ball can be made, if a shot would result in a legal hit, etc. To even ask a referee for a subjective opinion is considered to be poor manners by many players. At any time a referee may consult with other tournament officials for any reason they deem necessary -- i.e., rule interpretations, etc.

If you are not the match winner it is always considered good manners to shake your opponents hand without complaining about your loss or making excuses. It is telling your opponent that he or she did a good job. In professional play a serious breach of etiquette occurs in all of the following circumstances:

- Failure to attend a pre tournament player's meeting.

- Conceding balls during a game or match.

- Placing a hand in a pocket to catch a ball, catching a ball, or touching or in any way deliberately interfering with a ball as it enters a pocket.

- Use of tobacco products or alcoholic beverages during a match.

- Withdrawing from a tournament after the draw without good cause..

- Use of the player's guest pass by anyone who is not an immediate member of the player's family.

- Delay of the game (over one minute) between execution of shots.

- Failure to meet financial obligations in a timely manner. i.e., entry fees, hotel bills, car rentals, etc.

- Making or having others make statements that may, or can, bring the maker or the sport of billiards in disrepute.

- Taking or causing others to take action that may, or can, bring the taker or the sport of billiards in disrepute.

- Criticizing fellow professionals, tournament personnel, equipment, or facilities to the press or in public.

- Using abusive language, abusing equipment, or causing distractions of any kind during a match. Good sportsmanship during all matches is de-rigor.

- Blatant use of profane language during a match in a public area is not tolerated.

In professional play the conduct and ethics committee can fine and disqualify players who act or dress improperly.

Tournament etiquette

Don't brag about your skills and don't try to hustle less skilled players. There is always a better player lurking in the shadows who will take your money if your ego is large enough and you are stupid enough to let it take control.

Register and pay your tournament fees well ahead of time.

If you register for a tournament show up.

Know the rules of the pool game you will be playing and the rules that will be used in the tournament before the tournament begins.

Warm up before your match is scheduled to begin.

Be on time for your matches.

Dress properly. Conform to the dress code. (Check with the tournament director if you have questions.)

Before your match shake your opponent's hand and wish him/her luck.

After the match begins do not break your opponent's concentration or your concentration by talking with others.

Don't draw attention to yourself at anytime by yelling, banging or pounding your cue stick on the floor, or other childish behavior.

Do not use tactics that will distract or annoy your opponent or break his/her rhythm, attention, or concentration. This includes walking in front your opponent while he/she is lining up a shot, shouting at someone across the room, blowing tobacco smoke at them, or making sucking sounds with a straw in an empty soft drink container.

Don't try to have a conversation with your opponent while he/she is shooting.

Don't argue with your opponent about a rule or possible foul. Call the tournament director and accept the director's decision graciously.

Avoid bumping players at other tables at all times. If you do happen to bump another player apologize.

When you end your inning with a miss or a foul, sit down and stay seated and let your opponent shoot.

Call fouls on your opponent when they occur.

A referee's calls will stand in a tournament unless it is such a flagrant mistake that the tournament director reverses the decision. So don't complain about a bad call unless it gets the referee removed.

If a referee repeatedly makes bad calls during a tournament voice your concern to the tournament director and request the referee be replaced. Don't argue with the referee over questionable calls.

After a match shake hands with your opponent. If your opponent won give congratulations. If you won accept the congratulations offered graciously.

After the match don't complain about your bad rolls, your bad luck, or your opponents good luck.

Spectator Etiquette

Sports fans of any sport are not known for their good manners. There are many cases where the fans have attempted to influence the outcome of a competition between two teams. In the sport of billiards, use of the techniques described here can get you ejected from the spectator area.

Do not talk loudly to other spectators when a player is at the table. Speak softly. Loud conversations can be very distracting to players.

Do not shout across the room to another person during a match or tournament.

When rooting for a particular player do not applaud when the opponent fouls, makes a bad shot, or gets a bad roll..

Do not clap or cheer when a player makes a mistake or misses a shot.

Do not "boo" a player when a good shot is made.

As a spectator never try to "shark" a player.

Do not walk through the tournament area when matches are i n play. Specifically do not walk next to any table where tournament players are engaged in a match.

Do not play and personal matches on any table adjacent to a table being used for tournament play.

While it is often accepted to applaud when a good shot is made it is better for the player's concentration to save your applause for the end of a game or the end of the match.

The rules of etiquette for players apply equally to spectators.

Dress Codes

The dress codes associated with the play of pocket billiards are of particular interest to the serious student of the game.

Hustlers

Appropriate dress for the unknown hustler in a working class bar is that of a blue collar worker who just arrived in town or got off work. Blue jeans, work shirts, hard hats, and carpenters' overalls worn with work boots all fit the dress code of the hustler. In an upscale room the attire is casual clothing -- slacks and a polo shirt; and in some cases it can even be a suit or shirt and tie if business people are present.

Regular League Play

For the team or league player, normal street clothes are generally considered appropriate during *the regular league season*. Swim and beach wear for a man or woman is inappropriate. For a woman any type of suggestive clothing or clothing that might be construed as suggestive as well as skirts shorter than knee length are considered inappropriate.

For sanctioned play (*league tournaments*) the dress code for league play will often be as follows:

- Collared sport or dress shirt with sport or dress slacks.
- No tennis shoes of any kind.
- No shorts.
- No T-shirts.
- No jeans.
- No logos, designs, or advertising on shirt backs. Pocket logos only.
- The dress code is for both men and women and will be strictly enforced.

Of course the dress code for team and tournament play can vary from league to league. But if you follow the dress code used by the Billiard Congress of America you will be within the accepted norm. This dress code often serves as a model:

For team competition:

- Team shirts are mandatory. Matching designed shirts or collared shirts. No T-shirts.

- No shorts, cut-offs, ripped jeans, or swimwear. Dress slacks or skirts are preferred.

- Clean neat shoes. Use your best judgment.

- For individual competition.

- No shorts, cut-offs, tank tops, halter tops, swimwear, or sleeveless T-shirts.

- No suggestive clothing.

- Shoes must be worn at all times.

- All players will present themselves in a neat and clean appearance for their scheduled matches.

- Players not abiding by the dress code will be required to change clothes or withdraw from the tournament. The tournament officials have the right to ask any improperly attired player or spectator to leave the playing area.

Professional Play

The following dress codes are used by both the Men's Professional Billiard Association and the Woman's Professional Billiard Association.

Dress Code A: Formal

Men:

- Proper dress is Tuxedo and full vest or cummerbund, with formal patent leather or dress work shoes.

Women:

- Proper dress is tuxedo, knee length or longer evening gown, and formal wear (formal jump suits or coordinated suits are proper) of silk, satin, crepe, lace, faille, or metallic fabrics worn with leather dress shoes, and nylons or coordinated dress slack hose.

Dress Code B: Dress

Men:

- Suit with tie or sport jacket with dress trousers, dress shirt or dress sweater or polo sweater, and leather shoes with socks. A belt must be worn with slacks having belt loops.

Women:

- Dress slacks, skirts, culottes of linen, gabardine, wool, suiting, or challis worn with dress blouses or sweaters, leather or vinyl dress shoes, and nylons or dress slack hose. (Dresses worn should not be too revealing below the shoulder when bent over, nor too revealing above the knee in bending positions.)

- No cords, blue jeans, nor denim material. No plain cotton or similar shirts. No designer warm ups, sweats, nor shorts of any kind. No canvas shoes or sneaker type shoes.

Dress Code C: Casual

Men:

- Cotton slacks, cords, colored denims, polo shirts, designer shirts, leather or casual shoes only.

Women:

- Cotton slacks, colored denims, designer warm ups, polo shirts, cotton shirts, non-collared shirts in good taste, canvas or other casual shoes in good repair and appearance.

Dress Code Enforcement for General Tournament Play

Individual tournament directors determine what acceptable dress codes are for the players in the tournaments conducted by them. Because of this the dress codes will often seem to be arbitrary and capricious to an outsider. And it is in many cases. The tournament director can exclude any player that does not conform to the dress code set for the tournament. This is true in both amateur and professional play.

In a professional *prestige* event that is *to be televised* and because of the *poor image* that pool and billiards has had in the recent past there are those in the industry who believe if you force a person to dress in evening clothes that person automatically becomes more acceptable to the general public. Unfortunately it can also work to the detriment of the industry by portraying it as such a formal sport that the participants are not having fun and are uncomfortable in the clothes.

Dress codes: Enforcement -- Professionals

Any player who reports to a match and does not meet the required dress code will receive a verbal advisement from the Conduct and Ethics Committee. The player must then correct the fault and be ready to play in proper attire within the time limit specified in the warning or forfeit the match.

General:

The absolute minimum dress code at all professionally sanctioned events is dress code C and is in effect from check in at the tournament site through check out time or the equivalent. This includes the player's own personal time at any place even close to the tournament location. The committee on conduct and ethics must approve any deviation in public view from the dress code described above!

- Logos and Trademarks:

- Players may wear identifying trademarks and logos no larger than four inches (4") at the largest point of measurement when worn above the waist and no larger than two inches (2") at the largest point of measurement when worn below the waist.

- A player may not wear more than four (4) trademarks and/or logos on his/her person at the same time.

Tournament Play

Tournaments and tournament play are a very important part of pool and billiards but very little has been written about these subjects for the pool player.

When you are thinking about entering a tournament the first thing you need to consider is the size and type of table that will be used for tournament play. Games played on bar tables will be different from games played on non-bar tables. There will be differences in the cue ball weights, possible differences in the cue ball size, and differences in the pocket openings.

All of these differences can affect how you do in a tournament.

As an example, non-coin operated tables generally have a cue ball that is the same size and weight as the object balls,

On Valley pool tables the cue ball is roughly twice the weight of the object ball. The additional weight requires a stronger hit than a standard cue ball,

Dynamo pool tables use a cue ball that is almost three times heavier than the object balls. This cue ball not only requires a stronger hit but requires new skills to play proficiently.

Finally, on other types of coin operated tables the manufacturers simply use an oversize cue ball. This affects the play since the contact point between the object ball and cue ball is slight different than with a standard cue ball. This difference in contact point is obvious when an object ball is frozen on a rail and is played for the corner pocket along the rail.

While you are considering the tables you might as well think about the pockets. On coin operated tables the pockets tend to be larger than those on time pay tables. A quick way to check pocket size is see if you can slip two balls in a corner pocket without freezing together. If they do not freeze you know the pockets are larger than the typical room table. Side pockets tend to be 1/2 inch narrower than corner pockets. Professional table specifications state that corner pockets must be 4 1/2 to 5 inches wide at the largest opening of the jaws. You will also want to check for dips around the pockets that allow balls to fall in from slow shots where they would not normally be made.

The size of the table --3 X 6, 3 1/2 X 7, or 4 X 8 -- will also affect position play and scratches.

The speed of the table will affect your stroke. A table with old worn cloth suggests a slow table. A table with new felt and short nap suggests a fast table.

You check a table for level by using a very gentle center ball stroke along each long rail. If the ball rolls toward the rail the table bed is high. If the ball rolls toward the center of the table the center of the table is low.

The final check is for the cushions. A quick check requires you to place the cue ball on the long string half way between the center spot and the side pocket. Aim the cue ball into a long rail close to a corner pocket and very firmly stroke it. If the cue ball strikes seven cushions before coming to rest the rails have standard rebound characteristics. If the cue ball strikes more cushions then the rails are live. If the cue ball strikes fewer rails the cushions are dead.

Another check for the speed of the table and the rails is to place the cue ball at each diamond and shoot it into opposite diamond as if you were lagging for the break. This will identify any dead rails or dead spots on the rails.

Finally you will probably want to check the table's stability. For this place several balls from the rack at random on the table and bump the table with your hip. If the balls move the table is unstable.

The Player Meeting

The player meeting is used by the tournament director to match initial contestants, hold a Calcutta if there is one, make sure all players know and understand the dress code and rules used for the tournament.

Typical questions that might be asked at a player meeting are:

Is the unintentional contact of a piece of clothing, hand, mechanical bridge, etc. -- a foul?

If a player is late for match what is the penalty?

If the cue ball and object ball are frozen is it a push shot, a double hit, or a legal shot? (Can you play through the centers of the two balls?)

Is it permissible to use a ball not in play to measure the distance between two balls or one ball and the rail?

Is it just the blue denim color in jeans you dislike or is all denim clothing outlawed for the tournament?

Are jump shots legal?

Are masse shots legal?

Are balls made when the cue ball jumps off the table spotted or do they remain pocketed?

Can spectators call a foul on a player?

Can a player be given an out of headstring warning?

Can a spectator a coach player?

Tournament Structure

Every tournament player should have a minimum knowledge of the mechanics needed to organize and run a tournament.

Byes, seeding principles, and tournament structure is seldom discussed by tournament players. The reason for having a bye is that an insufficient number of people registered for the tournament to provide for a smooth flow of competition. They are necessary when there are not enough competitors to fill all the slots for the first round of competition.

Byes are assigned on the tournament board starting at the bottom of the board. They should be assigned so the better competitors are not eliminated in the early rounds of the competition. Byes are placed at opposite ends of each bracket so that an equal number of byes will be placed in each quadrant of the initial competition.

Seeding is performed regardless of whether or not byes must be assigned. The purpose of seeding is to have the best players at opposite ends of the tournament board so they have the best opportunity to meet in the final competition. Generally speaking the top seeded competitors should be matched against the lowest rated players in the first round of a tournament.

There are a number of ways of structuring tournaments. The ones most common in pool and billiards are round robins, single elimination, and double elimination. But don't be lulled into believing these are the best or the only ways of structuring tournaments. They are used because they are the most expedient, not because they most accurately determine the best competitors.

The round robin tournament requires each competitor to play all other competitors. It has a great advantage over other types of tournament structures because competitors are not eliminated until all competitors have played each other. The problem with the round robin is the number of matches that need to be played as the number of competitors grows. For example, for a 32 competitor field 496 matches would need to be played. Time constraints and table availability eliminate strict use of this type of tournament. When large numbers of are involved and a round robin format is used, the competitors are divided into sections of six or eight competitors and the top winners of each section advance to the next stage in the competition. (Kinda sounds like league competition in the big city doesn't it?)

The single elimination tournament is the fastest and easiest to administer. However, it discourages the better competitors from entering the competition since they can meet stiff competition early on. The single elimination tournament involves the elimination of all participants except the one who wins.

Finally, there is the double elimination tournament that all experienced tournament pool players are familiar with. The underlying reason for a double elimination tournament, other than allowing a contestant two defeats before being eliminated, is to prevent the better contestants from eliminating each other before reaching the finals or having to play each other a second time too soon.

With the double elimination tournament the winning competitors continue to play winners until there are no more winners left to play. The losers on the other hand play other losers until there is only one competitor with a single loss. This competitor then plays the competitor with no losses. If the competitor with no losses wins the match is over. If the competitor with no losses loses -- a second match is played and the winner of that match is declared the winner of the tournament.

The Calcutta

A Calcutta is a form of gambling that has been used to place bets on major sporting events for years.

The most visible and popular individual sport competition where Calcutta's have been used in recent years is in golf. (Frequently at country clubs where there is money to be made by conning the rich membership.)

Specifically, a Calcutta is a limited form of betting which combines elements from a lottery with elements from traditional book making. In many states a Calcutta is not legal. In some states it is. In most state there are lobbying groups attempting to influence the lawmakers to pass laws to legalize the Calcutta as well as other forms of gambling.

A Calcutta is supposed to be run by an auctioneer who has no financial interest in the outcome of the event. The Calcutta begins after the participants in the tournament have been identified. (In the case of an open pool tournament this would be when the tournament registration is closed.)

The timing of the auction may be the day the tournament begins or the Calcutta may be held the evening before play begins.

The Calcutta opens as a player auction in which gamblers bid for individual participants. The bids for the privilege of "owning" a participant depends on the level of the tournament and knowledge of the skill levels of each player in the tournament. As an example local amateur tournaments may be lucky to generate a total pot of $500.00 while a major professional tournament in Las Vegas could create a Calcutta pot of $200,00 or more.

In some areas of the country players are allowed to "purchase a portion of themselves from their owner."

The auctioneer generally skims 5-20% of the proceeds as the auction fee. Another 10% of the proceeds may go to a designated charity. The remainder is typically divided up as follows:

50% to the holder of the first place player

20% to the holder of the second place player

15% to the holder of the third place player

10% to the holder of the fourth place player

5% to the holder of the fifth place player

At the completion of the tournament it is customary for the owners of each of the players winning money in the Calcutta to reward their player with 10% of their winnings.

A variation in the auction can be made by auctioning off the tournament finish places instead of individual players. By auctioning an individual place the winning bidder is allowed to select or designate the participant or player for that place. This allows all participants in a tournament to be included in the Calcutta by placing all unchosen players in the final Calcutta category.

The mechanics of the Calcutta require all winning bids to be immediately deposited with the auctioneer in cash. Each winning bidder receives a card or receipt for his deposit showing the name of the participant selected, the amount of the deposit, and the total amount in the pool. The money in the pool, less the auctioneers' fees and commissions is paid out at the competition of the tournament in accordance with the published or publicized fee schedule.

In a tournament that takes several days to compete gamblers who "own" players frequently resort to hedging and scalping their player in an attempt to make money on their player regardless of where he finishes in the tournament. Sometimes they are able to sell shares in a player that's up to several times their auction bid.

Hundreds of Calcutta auctions are run in association with local and regional pool tournaments every year. Many of the first prize awards in these contests are won by hustlers that pose as poor players and then play top grade pool and walk off with the first prize. It is usually a good idea to look suspiciously at a new pool player entering a tournament where a Calcutta is involved. He may be a ringer.

At the other end of the spectrum is the player who can be bribed to throw a match. It is easy enough for any pool player to "miss" a shot and lose the match to collect a bribe worth more than the tournament first prize.

The gimmicks of hustling and ringers are used all the time by golf hustlers who prey on country club golfers. It is not unusual for a hustler to work several locations at the same time.

The best advice is don't participate in a Calcutta if you don't know all the players.

GENERAL RULES OF POCKET BILLIARDS

The rules listed here are those that apply to billiards games in general. These rules generally apply to all games, *unless* specifically noted to the contrary in the individual game rules.

To facilitate the use and understanding of these general rules, terms that may require definition are set in *italics* so that the reader may refer to the glossary section for the exact meaning for the word.

For purposes of simplicity and clarity, the masculine pronouns have been used throughout the book. These terms apply to any and all players or teams of players.

Tables, Balls And Other Equipment. All games described in this book are designed for play on any of the standardized table sizes. Generally this is a table with a width that is one half of the length. Some sizes are 4' x 8'; 4 1/2' x 9'; 5' x 10'.

Striking The Cue Ball Legal shots require that the cue ball be struck only with the cue tip. Failure to meet this requirement is a foul.

Lag For Break The following procedure is used for the *lag* for the opening break. Each player should use a cue ball that is the same size and weight. If these are not available solid object balls can be used. With the balls in had behind the *head string*, one player to the left and one to the right of the *head spot*, the balls are shot simultaneously to the *foot* cushion so that the cue rebounds to the head end of the table. The player whose ball is the closest to the innermost edge of the head cushion wins the lag. The lagged ball must touch the foot cushion at least once. Other cushion contacts are immaterial, except as prohibited below.

It is an automatic loss of the lag if 1) the ball crosses into the opponent's half of the table, or 2)the balls fails to contact the foot cushion, or 3) the ball drops into a pocket, or 4) the ball *jumps* the table. If both players violate the automatic loss of lag rules, and there is no referee or the referee is unable to determine which ball would be closer, the lag is replayed.

Opening Break Shot The opening break shot is determined by either the lag or the *lot*. (The lag for break procedure is required for tournament and other formal competitions.) The player winning the lag or lot has the choice of performing the opening break shot or passing it to the opponent.

The Cue Ball On Opening Break *The opening break shot is taken with cue ball in hand behind the head string.* The object balls are *racked* or positioned according to the specific game rules.

Cue Ball In Hand Behind The Head String When the cue ball is *in hand behind the head string*, it remains in hand (not in play) until the player drives the cue ball out of the *kitchen* by striking it with his cue tip; or in the referee's judgment touches it with any part of the cue in a*n obvious attempt* to perform a shot.

The cue ball may be *adjusted* by the player's hand, cue, etc., so long as it remains in hand. Once the cue ball is in play it may not be impeded in any way by the player; to do so is to commit a foul.

Pocketed Balls A ball is considered as a pocketed ball if as a result of an otherwise legal shot, it drops of the bed of the table into the pocket and remains there. A ball that rebounds from the pocket back onto the table bed is not a pocketed ball. (A ball that falls out of a ball return system onto the floor, or falls out of the pocket to the floor remains a pocketed ball.)

Position Of Balls The position of a ball is judged by where it's base, point of contact with the table, or center rests.

Foot On The Floor It is a foul if a player shoots when at least one foot is not in contact with the floor. Foot attire must be normal in regard to size, shape and manner in which it is worn.

Shooting With Balls In Motion It is a foul if a player shoots while the cue ball or any object ball is in motion. (A spinning ball is considered to be in motion.)

Completion Of Stroke A stroke is not complete (and therefore is not counted) until all balls on the table have become motionless after the stroke. (A spinning ball is considered to be in motion.)

Kitchen Defined The Head String is not part of the kitchen. Thus an object that is dead center on the head string line is playable when specific game rules require that a player must shoot at a ball outside the kitchen. Likewise, the cue ball when being put in play from the kitchen (ball in hand behind the string)may not be placed directly on the head string line, it must be behind it.

All Fouls General Though the penalties for fouls differ from game to game, the following apply to all fouls 1) the player's inning ends, and 2) if on a stroke, the stroke is invalid and any pocketed balls are not counted to the shooter's credit.

Foul By Touching A Ball Unless otherwise stated, it is a foul to strike, touch or in any way make contact with the cue ball in play or any object balls in play with anything except the cue tip (while the cue tip is attached to the cue stick). Contact by the body, clothing, chalk, mechanical bridge, cue shaft or other extraneous items is considered to be a foul.

Foul By Double Hit It is a foul if the cue ball is struck more than once on a shot by the cue tip. (Such shots are usually referred to as double hits)If, in the referee's judgment, the cue ball has felt initial contact with the cue tip and then is struck a second time in the course of the same stroke, it is a foul.*

(*This can be very difficult for the referee to judge, because on shots where the distance between the cue ball and the object ball is very short, it must be judged whether the cue ball had time to move out of contact with the cue tip prior to striking the object ball and rebounding and being struck with the cue tip a second time. If it is judged, by sound; by ball position and action; by the stroke used, that there were two separate contacts of the cue ball by the cue tip on a stroke, the stroke is a foul and must be called as a foul.)

Push Shot Foul It is a foul if the cue ball is pushed by the cue tip, with contact being maintained for more that the momentary time commensurate with a stroked shot. Such shots are usually referred to as a *push shot.* If the referee judges that the player laid the cue tip against the cue ball and them pushed on into a shot, maintaining contact beyond the normal momentary split-second, the stroke is a foul and must be called as a foul.

Player Responsibility Foul The player is responsible for chalk, bridges, files, and any other items or equipment he brings to, uses at or near the table. If a player drops a piece of chalk on the table bed and it strikes any ball it is a foul. If when using a mechanical bridge, the bridge comes in contact with any ball it is a foul. The same applies to the player's clothing. i.e.,-- If a sleeve of a shirt comes in contact with any of the balls it is a foul.

Cue Ball Jumped Off Table When a stroke causes the cue ball to leave the table it is considered to be a foul. A *Jumped* object ball may or may not be a foul, that is determined by the specific game rules.

Illegal Jumping Of Ball It is a foul if a player strikes the cue ball below center ("digs under" it) and intentionally causes it to rise off the bed of the table in an effort to clear an obstructing ball. Such jumping action may occasionally occur accidentally, and such jumps are not to be considered fouls of their face; they may still be ruled foul strokes, if the ferrule or cue shaft makes contact with the cue ball in the course of the shot.

Jump Shots Unless otherwise stated in the rules for a specific game it is legal to cause the cue ball to rise off the bed of the table by elevating the cue stick on the shot (masse) and forcing the cue ball to rebound from the bed of the table.

Balls Jumped Off Table Balls coming to rest on surfaces other that the bed of the table after a stroke (i.e. the cushion top, the rail surface, the floor, etc.) are considered jumped balls. Balls may bounce on the cushion tops, rails or light fixtures above the table in play without being jumped balls if they return to the bed of the table under their own power and without touching anything not a part of the table equipment. The table equipment shall consist of its light fixture, chalk not on the bed of the table, and any of the permanent parts of the table proper. Balls that strike or touch anything not a part of the table equipment shall be considered jumped balls even though they might return to the bed of the table after contacting the non equipment item(s).

All jumped object balls are spotted when all balls have stopped moving. See specific game rules to determine whether a jumped object ball is a foul. A cue ball jumped off the table is a foul; see specific game rules for putting the cue ball in play after a jumped cue ball foul.

Special Intentional Foul Penalty The cue ball in play shall not be intentionally struck with anything other than tip portion of a cue. (Not the ferrule, shaft, butt, etc.) Such actions are considered fouls. If the referee deems that the contact was intentional, the player shall be warned one time during the match that a second violation during that match will result in the loss of the match. If a second violation occurs the match is forfeited.

One Foul Limit Unless specific game rules dictates otherwise, only one foul is assessed on a player in each inning. If different penalties can apply, the most sever penalty is the factor determining which foul is assessed.

Balls Moving Spontaneously If a ball shifts, settles, turns or otherwise moves "by itself," the ball shall remain in the position it assumed and play continues. A hanging ball that falls into a pocket "by itself" after being motionless for 5 seconds or longer shall be replaced as closely as possible to it's position prior to falling, and play shall continue.

If an object ball drops into a pocket "by itself" as a player shoots at it, so that the cue ball passes over the spot the ball had been on, unable to miss it, the cue ball and object ball are replaced to their original positions and the player must execute the shot again. Any other object balls disturbed on the stroke are also to be replaced to their original positions for the shot to be replayed.

Spotting Balls When specific game rules call for spotting balls, they shall be replaced on the table on the long string after the stroke is complete. A single ball is placed on the foot spot. If more than one ball is to be spotted, they are placed on the long string in ascending numerical order, beginning on the foot spot and advancing toward the foot rail.

When balls on or near the foot spot or long string interfere with the spotting of balls, the balls to be spotted are placed on the long string as close as possible to the foot spot without moving the interfering balls. Spotted balls are to be *frozen* to such interfering balls, except when the cue ball is interfering. Balls that are to be spotted against the cue ball are placed as close as possible without being frozen.

If there is insufficient room on the long string between the foot spot and the foot rail cushion for balls that must be spotted, such balls are then placed on the extension of the long string *in front* of the foot spot (between the foot spot and the center spot), as near as possible to the foot spot and in the same numerical order as if they were spotted behind the foot spot. (Example: If the two ball and the fourteen ball are to be spotted the fourteen would be closest to the foot spot then the two ball next to it.)

Jawed Balls/Locked Balls If two or more balls are locked between the *jaws* or sides of the pocket, with one or more suspended in air, the referee shall inspect the balls in position and follow this procedure: He shall visually (or physically if he desires) project each ball directly downward from it's locked position. Any ball that in his judgment would fall in the pocket if moved directly downward is pocketed. Any ball that would rest on the bed of the table is not pocketed. The balls are then placed according to the referee's decision and play continues according to the specific game rules.

Additional Pocketed Balls If a player completes a legal, scoring stroke on which an object ball or balls in addition to the intended, called, required or designated ball or balls also drop, such additional balls shall be counted, credited and scored in accordance with the scoring rules for the specific game. There are some games that negate this rule.

Non-Player Interference If the balls are moved (or the table is bumped so that play is directly affected) by a non-player during a match, the balls shall be replaced as near as possible to their original positions immediately prior to the incident, and play shall resume with no penalty on the player affected. If the match is officiated, the referee shall replace the balls. This rule shall also apply to "act of God" interference, such as earthquake, hurricane, tornado, light fixture falling, power failure, etc. If the balls cannot be restored to their original positions, replay the game with the original player breaking.

Breaking Subsequent Racks When *short rack games* are being completed in a format requiring sets or races, the winner of each game breaks the next rack. The following are common options that may be designated 1) players alternate break 2) loser breaks 3) player trailing in games/score breaks the next game.

Play By Innings Unless individual game rules specify differently, players alternate turns (innings) at the table, with a player's inning ending when he either fails to legally pocket a ball or fouls.

Object Ball Frozen To Cushion Or Cue Ball This rule applies to any shot where the cue ball's first contact with a ball is with one that is frozen to a cushion or to the cue ball itself. After the cue ball makes contact with the frozen object ball, the shot must result in either 1) a ball being pocketed; or 2) the cue ball contacting a cushion; or 3) the frozen ball being caused to contact a cushion (not just rebounding from the cushion it was frozen to); or 4) another object ball being caused to contact a cushion to which it was not already in contact with. Failure to satisfy one of these four requirements is a foul. Some games have additional requirements.

Playing From Behind The String When a player has the cue ball in hand behind the head string (in the kitchen), he must drive the cue ball to a point outside the kitchen before it contacts either a cushion or an object ball. Failure to do so is either a foul, or at the opponent's option, the shooting player can be required to replay the shot after the balls have been replaced to their original positions. If the second option is chosen there is not foul.

EIGHT BALL

Introduction: Eight ball is considered an amateur game by the professionals. It is the game played in bars and taverns around the United States in some form, wherever coin operated tables are in use. In many places it is the only game the local players have ever played. As the game of choice it has many local variations as the English language has. The standard rules of eight ball are given below. The variations of the game are endless. The more common variations are provided in the next section.

These rules apply except when clearly contradicted by the General Rules of Pocket Billiards.

OBJECT OF THE GAME:

Eight ball is played with a cue ball and fifteen object balls, numbered 1 through 15. One player must pocket balls of the group numbered 1 through 7 (solids), while the other player has 9 through 15 (stripes). The player that pocket all of their group of balls and then legally pockets the 8-ball wins the game.

THE RACK:

The balls are racked in a triangle at the foot of the table with the 8-ball in the center of the triangle, the first ball of the rack is placed on the foot spot, a stripe ball in one corner of the rack and a solid ball in the other corner.

ALTERNATING BREAK:

Winner of coin toss has option to break. During individual competition, players will alternate breaking on each subsequent game.

LEGAL BREAK SHOT:

With the cue ball behind the head string, the breaker must either 1) pocket a ball, or 2) drive four numbered balls to the rail. If a legal break is not made IT IS NOT A FOUL. However the incoming player has the option of 1) accepting the table in position and shooting. or 2) having the balls re-racked and shooting the opening break himself. It is not necessary to hit the head ball (the ball that is on the foot spot) to initiate a legal break in 8-ball.

SCRATCH ON A LEGAL BREAK:

If a player scratches on a legal break shot 1) all balls pocketed are spotted including the 8-ball, 2) IT IS A FOUL, 3) the table is open.

PLEASE NOTE:

The incoming player has cue ball in hand behind the headstring and may not shoot an object ball that is behind the headstring, unless he first shoots the cue ball past the headstring and then by hitting a rail causes the cue ball to come back behind the headstring and hit the object ball.

8-BALL POCKETED ON THE BREAK:

If the 8-ball is pocketed on the break, the breaker may ask for a re-rack or have the 8-ball spotted and continue shooting. If the breakers scratches while pocketing the 8-ball on the break, the incoming players has the option of a re-rack or having the 8-ball spotted and begin shooting with ball in hand behind the headstring.

HEADSTRING RULE:

This rule applies only when the opening player scratches on the break, and the incoming player has ball in hand behind the headstring. The incoming players may place the cue ball anywhere behind the headstring. If the players places the cue ball on or in front of the headstring and shoots, it is a foul. He may shoot at any object ball as long as the base of the object ball is on or past the headstring. He may not shoot at any ball whose base is behind the headstring, unless he first shoots the cue ball past the headstring and then by hitting a rail causes the cue ball to come back behind the headstring and hit the object ball.

The base of the ball (the point of the ball touching the table) determines whether a ball is within or without of the headstring. If the incoming player inadvertently places the cue ball in front of the headstring, it is a good gesture for his opponent to inform him before he shoots to avoid confusion.

OPEN TABLE:

The table is open when the choice of groups(stripes or solids has not yet been determined. When the table is open, it is legal to hit any ball. *THE TABLE IS ALWAYS OPEN IMMEDIATELY FOLLOWING THE BREAK.* When the table is open it is legal to hit any solid or stripe or the 8-ball in the process of pocketing the called ball. On an open table, all illegally pocketed balls are spotted.

CHOICE OF GROUP:

The choice of stripes or solids *IS NOT DETERMINED ON THE BREAK EVEN IF BALLS ARE MADE FROM ONLY ONE GROUP OR BOTH GROUPS.* The choice of balls is only determined when a player legally pockets a called object ball after the break shot.

LEGAL SHOT:

On all shots (except the break and when the table is open, the shooter must hit one of his group of balls first and, either 1) pocket an object ball, or 2) cause the cue ball or any object ball to contact a rail.

NOTE: It is okay for the shooter to bank the cue ball off a rail before contacting his object ball. However, after contact with his object ball, an object ball must be pocketed, or the cue ball or any object ball must contact a rail.

SAFETY PLAY:

Safety play is defined as a legal shot. If the shooting players intends to play safe by pocketing an obvious object ball, the prior to the shot, he must declare a safety to his opponent. If this is not done, the shooter will be required to shoot again. The shooter's object balls considered illegally pocketed and must be spotted.

SCORING:

A player is entitle to continue shooting until he fails to legally pocket a ball of his group. After a player has legally pocketed all of his group of balls he shoots to pocket the 8-ball.

FOULS:

The following infractions result in fouls:

    a. Failure to execute a legal shot as defined above.

    b. A scratch shot (shooting the cue ball into a pocket or off the table.).

    c. A scratch shot on a legal break.

    d. Shooting without at least one foot touching the floor.

    e. Moving or touching the cue ball in any fashion be means other than legal play is a foul.

    f. Shooting a jump shot over another ball by scooping the cue stick under the cue ball is illegal and a foul. A jump shot executed by **striking the cue ball** above center is legal.

    PLEASE NOTE: A player does not commit a foul when he accidentally miscues and causes the ball to jump above the surface of the table.

    g. In organized competition (league or tournament play) if a team member advises or coaches another team member who is the shooter at the time, it is a foul on the team member shooting.

FOUL PENALTY:

Opposing player gets cue ball in hand. This means that the player can place the cue ball anywhere on the table (*it does not have to be behind the headstring except on the opening break*). This rule prevents a player from making intentional fouls which would put his opponent at a disadvantage. With cue ball in hand, the player may position the cue ball on the table by hand (*more than once if necessary*). After placing the cue ball, the shaft and ferrule of the cue stick (*not the tip*) may also be used for positioning the cue ball for shooting.

COMBINATION SHOTS:

Combination shots are allowed. The 8-ball cannot be used as a first ball in the combination except when the table is open.

ILLEGALLY POCKETED BALLS:

An object ball is considered to be illegally pocketed when

> 1) that object ball is pocketed on the same shot a foul is committed, or
>
> 2) the called ball did not go in the designated pocket, or
>
> 3) a safety is called prior to the shot.

If playing on a regular table the balls are spotted. If play is on a coin operated table the pocketed balls remain off the table.

SPOTTING BALLS:

Whenever an object ball is to be spotted, the object ball is spotted on the long string as close the foot spot as possible and shall be frozen to any interfering ball except the cue ball. The balls are spotted in numerical order starting with the lowest number ball.

OBJECT BALL JUMPED OFF THE TABLE:

If any object ball is jumped off the table, it is a miss and loss of turn, not a foul, unless it is the 8-ball, which is a loss of the game. The shooter's object ball is spotted and any of the opponent's jumped balls will be pocketed.

OBJECT BALL FROZEN TO RAIL:

This rule applies when the object ball to be struck by the cue ball is frozen to the rail. After the cue ball contacts the object ball you must

    1) pocket the frozen ball or any other object ball, or

    2) drive the frozen object ball to another cushion,

    or 3) drive the cue ball or another object ball to any cushion.

Failure to do so is a foul. When there is any doubt whether the object ball is frozen to a cushion, the players should ask for a ruling before shooting.

DOUBLE HIT:

If the cue ball is touching your object ball prior to the shot, the player may shoot towards it with a level cue, providing that his cue stick strikes rather than pushes the cue ball. If the cue ball is close, but not froze to the object ball, the cue must be elevated to a 45 degree angle when shooting in the general direction of the line of the two balls. A level cue may be used if aiming 45 degrees or more off the line of the two balls.

PLAYING THE 8-BALL:

When shooting at the 8-ball, a scratch or foul is not loss of game if the 8-ball is not pocketed or jumped from the table. The incoming player has ball in hand.

LOSS OF GAME:

A player loses the game if he commits any of the following infractions:

    a. Fouls when pocketing the 8-ball. EXCEPTION: See 8-ball pocketed on the break.

    b. Pockets the 8-ball on the same stroke as the last of his group of balls.

    c. Jumps the 8-ball off the table at any time.

    d. Pockets the 8-ball in a pocket other that the one called.

    e. Pockets the 8-ball when it is not the legal object ball.

STALEMATED GAME:

If in 3 consecutive turns at the table by each player (6 turns total), they purposely foul or scratch and both players agree that attempting to pocket or move an object ball will result in immediate loss of game, then the game will be considered a stalemate. The balls will then be re-racked and the breaker of the stalemated game will break again.

NOTE: Three consecutive fouls by one players is not a loss of game.

DISQUALIFICATION:

In league or tournament play the league or tournament director has the right to disqualify any player from competition and the player forfeits the right to prize money and/or any other awards for unsportsmanlike conduct or tactics detrimental to the league or tournament.

SPECTATOR COACHING:

Spectators on the sidelines should not be allowed to advise or coach a player during competition. if after asking a spectator not to coach a player and he continues to do so the referee should ask the spectator to leave the tournament area.

PLEASE NOTE:

Any place in the rules that states to spot an illegally pocketed ball will only apply if the table is not designed for coin operation.

EIGHT BALL VARIATIONS

Eight ball is played with various sets of rules depending on where you play. In some areas of the country all balls pocketed must be called. In other areas the only ball that is called in the eight ball. The rule variations also depend on the type of table you are playing on. Obviously it is not practical to spot illegally pocketed balls on a coin operated table. With this in mind, the following variations in the rules of eight ball are given.

CALL SHOT ALSO KNOWN AS STRAIGHT CALL SHOT

In call shot the pocket where the object ball will be made and the number of the object ball to be pocketed there must be designated. Failure to pocket the designated object ball in the called pocket results in the loss of turn for the shooter.

In some locations the use of the call is carried to ridiculous lengths by disallowing any pocketed ball when the call did not include touching a rail prior to entering the pocket or kissing the object ball off another ball. This is really an attempt to keep a good player from effectively competing with a semiprofessional or professional who can and does make these calls for a living.

GENTLEMEN'S CALL SHOT

In Gentlemen's Call Shot call of obvious balls and pockets do not have to be indicated. It is the opponents right to ask which ball and pocket if he is unsure of the shot. Banks and combinations are not considered obvious and both the object ball and pocket must be called. When calling the shot, it is *NEVER* necessary to indicate details such as the number of cushions, banks, kisses, caroms, etc. If the object ball is not legally pocketed and other object balls are pocketed, the shooter's balls that were pocketed would be spotted and any of the opponent's balls remain pocketed. However, if play is on a coin operated table all balls would remain pocketed.

LAST POCKET

In this variation of the game the eight ball must be pocketed in the same pocket the last legally pocketed ball of your set. Pocketing the eight ball in any other pocket is a loss of the game.

ONE AND FIFTEEN

In this game the one and fifteen must be pocketed in designated side pockets. In the rack the one and fifteen are placed in the row directly behind the eight ball in the inside positions. The balls are placed in the rack on opposite the side of the table where they must be pocketed. For each set the one and fifteen act as free balls and can be pocketed at any time and immediately placed on the foot spot without the shooter ending his inning.

SCRATCHES

Another variation in the rules that frequently pops up is what happens when the cue ball is pocketed. In some locations the house rules state you spot a ball for the scratch. If you made a ball you may also be required to spot that ball too.

NINE BALL

SUMMARY

Nine ball is played with nine object balls numbered one through nine and a cue ball. On each shot the first ball the cue ball contacts must be the lowest numbered ball on the table, but the balls need not be pocketed in order. If a player pockets any ball on a legal shot, he remains at the table for another shot, and continues until he misses, fouls, or wins the game by pocketing the nine ball. After a miss, the incoming player must shoot from the position left by the previous player. After a foul the incoming player may start with the cue ball anywhere on the table. Certain *serious fouls* are penalized by loss of the game. Players are not required to call any shot. A match ends when one of the players has won the required number of games.

Detailed rules for nine ball are given below, followed by the definitions of some technical terms. These rules do not cover specifications of tables and balls, sanctioning conditions, or the handling of prize funds.

BEGINNING PLAY

Break

Order of play for the first game is determined by lag. The winner of the lag may break the first rack or assign the break to his opponent. In subsequent games of the match the a winner of the previous game will break.

Racking the Balls

The object balls are racked in a diamond shape, with the one balls at the top of the diamond and on the foot spot, the nine ball in the center of the diamond, and the other balls in arbitrary order. If the one ball is not touching both of the adjacent balls, the breaker may ask the referee to rerack the balls prior to the break. The cue ball begins in hand above the head string.

Break Shot

The rules governing the break sot are the same as for other shots except:

a) If the cue ball is pocketed or driven off the table, and no other foul is committed the incoming player has cue ball in hand above the head string. If the one ball is not below the head string, it is spotted on the long string. The incoming player may pass the shot after a scratch on the break, and the breaker must then shoot with ball in had above the head string.

b) The breaker must attempt an "open break" -- he must attempt to pocket a ball. Failure to do so is a standard foul.

c) If the breaker fails to contact the one ball, it is not considered a foul, the balls are reracked (if necessary), and the breaker breaks again, starting from behind the head string.

d) On the shot immediately following a legal break, the shooter may play a *"push out."* (See *Shot, Inning, Game, Match*)

CONTINUING PLAY

If the breaker pockets one or more balls on a legal break, he continues to shoot until he misses, fouls, or winds the game. If the player misses or fouls, the other player begins his inning and shoots until he misses, fouls, or wins. The game ends when the nine ball is pocketed on a legal shot, or the game is forfeited for a serious infraction of the rules.

STANDARD FOULS

Scratch

Pocketing the cue ball or driving it off the table is a foul.

Bad Hit

If the first object ball contacted by the cue ball is not the lowest numbered ball on the table, the shot is a foul.

No Rail

If no object ball is pocketed, failure to drive the cue ball or some object ball to a rail after the cue ball contacts the object ball is a foul.

Foot

Failure to have at least one foot in contact with the floor at the moment the cue tip contacts the cue ball is a foul.

Moving Ball

Shooting while *any* ball is moving or spinning is a foul.

Push Shot or Double Stroke

If the cue ball is touching the lowest numbered ball prior to the shot, the player may shoot towards it, providing that the cue stick strikes rather than pushed the cue ball. (The PBA has not yet adopted a rule covering the situation when the cue ball is close to but not touching the object ball.)

Touched Object Ball

It is a foul to touch a moving ball or allow that ball to hit any foreign object, such as a cube of chalk. (The top of the rail is not considered to be a foreign object.) It is not a foul to accidentally touch stationary object balls while in the act of shooting. If such an accident occurs, the players should allow the referee to restore the object balls to their correct positions. If the player does not allow such a restoration, and a ball set in motion as a normal part of the shoot touches such an unrestored ball, or passes partly into a region originally occupied by a disturbed ball, the shot is a foul. In short, if the accident has any effect on the outcome of the shot it is a foul. In any case, the referee must restore the positions of the disturbed balls as soon as possible, but not during the shot. It is a foul to play another shot before the referee has restored any accidentally moved balls.

At the non shooting player's option the disturbed balls will be left in their new positions. In this case, the balls are considered restored, and subsequent contact on them is not a foul.

Placement

Touching any object ball with the cue ball while it is in hand is a foul.

Object Ball

Players may touch object balls only to assist the referee in his duties. If a player intentionally touches any object ball for any other purposes while a game is in progress, whether that object ball is in play or not, he has fouled. (This rule does not apply to the usual collisions between the balls.)

Cue Ball

Except for ball in hand placement, if a player touches the cue ball with anything other than the chalked surface of his cue tip, he has fouled. The player may place the cue ball with anything other than the chalked surface of his cue tip.

Scoop Shot

If a player plays a shot with extreme draw with the intention of miscuing to make the cue ball jump over some obstruction, he has fouled. (See *Jump Shots*) Any miscue when executing a jump shot is a foul.

Interference

If the non shooting player distracts his opponent or interferes with his play, he has fouled. If a player shoots out of turn, or moves any ball except during his inning, it is considered to be interference.

Devices

Using any device in an uncustomary manner in lining up or executing a shot is a foul.

Practice

While a game is in progress, practice is not allowed. Taking a shot that is not part of that game is a foul.

SERIOUS FOULS

The following *serious fouls* are penalized by the loss of one game. if the referee has warned the player before the foul. If the referee fails to warn the player, any foul is penalized like a *standard foul*, except as noted.

Three Consecutive Fouls

If a play; fouls three times without making an intervening legal shot, he loses the game. The three fouls must occur in one game. The warning must be given between the second and third fouls.

Assistance

While a match is in progress, players are not allowed to ask spectators for assistance in planning or executing shots. If a player asks for and receives such assistance, he loses the game. Any spectator who spontaneously offers any significant help to a player will be removed from the area. (See *Before the Match*.)

Failure to Leave the Table

If a player does not stop shooting as soon as the referee has called a foul, he loses the game. The calling of the foul is considered to be the referee's warning to the player.

Slow Play

If the referee feels a player is playing exceptionally slowly, he must warn the player that he risks loss of a game if such slow play continues. Subsequently, if the referee and the tournament director agree that his play remains unacceptably slow, they may penalize the player one game for each game in which such slow play continues. (In general, no shot should take more than two minutes to plan and execute.)

Head String

After a scratch on a break shot, the cue ball is in hand above the head string. The referee should say, "Above the head string," when he hands the cue ball to the player, which constitutes the warning. If the player intentionally places the cue ball below the head string he loses the game. If the player accidentally places the cue ball slightly below the head string the referee must warn him again, or no foul is considered to have occurred. With cue ball in hand above the head string, if the player plays directly on an object ball above the head string with the cue ball first crossing the head string he loses the game. No warning is required in this last case.

Suspended Play

If a players shoots while play is suspended by the referee, he loses the game. Announcement of the suspension is considered sufficient warning.

Concession

If a player concedes, he loses the game. The unscrewing of a jointed cue stick, except to replace a shaft, is considered to be a concession. No warning from the referee is required in the case of a concession.

OTHER SITUATIONS AND INTERPRETATIONS

Outside Interference

When outside interference occurs during a shot that has an effect on the outcome of that shot, the referee will restore the balls to the positions they had before the shot, and the shot will be replayed. If the interference had no effect on the shot, the referee will restore the disturbed balls and play will continue.

Settling into Place

A ball may settle slightly after it appears to have stopped, possibly due to slight imperfections in the ball or the table. Unless this causes a ball to fall into a pocket, it is considered a normal hazard of play, and the ball will not be moved back. If a ball falls into a pocket as the result of such settling, it is replaced as close as possible to its original position. If a balls falls into a pocket during or just prior to a shot, and has an effect on the shot, the referee will restore the position and the shot will be replayed. Players are not penalized for shooting while a ball is settling.

Jump Shots

It is legal to cause the cue ball to rise off the bed of the table by elevating the cue stick on the shot,, and forcing the cue ball to rebound from the bed of the table. (See *Scoop Shots*)

Protesting Fouls

If a player thinks that the referee has failed to call a foul, he must protest to the referee before the next shot starts. If he fails to do so, and the foul goes unpenalized, the foul is considered not to have occurred. The referee is the final judge on matters of fact. If either player thinks the referee is applying the rules incorrectly, and the dispute cannot be resolved by reference to the rules, the referee must take the protest to the tournament director or his appointed substitute. The tournament director's decision on interpretation of the rules is final. A player may also protest if he thinks that the referee has called a foul incorrectly. In any case play is suspended until the protest is resolved.

Prompting Warnings

When a player thinks that the referee is failing to issue a mandatory warning, he remind the referee that such a warning is necessary.

Waiving Specific Rules

Prior to the start of the tournament, the tournament director may choose to waive or modify specific rules, e.g. the loser of a game rather than the winner may break the following games.

Late Start

A player must be ready to begin a match within fifteen minutes of the start of the match, or his opponent wins by forfeit. The starting time is considered to be the scheduled time or the time the match is announced, whichever is later.

Unsportsmanlike Conduct

If the referee and the tournament director agree that a player is persistently behaving in a disruptive or unsportsmanlike manner, they may penalize him in any way they choose, including calling a foul on him, awarding the game or match to his opponent, or forfeiting all of his remaining matches.

Texas Express 9-Ball Rules

Texas express is a variation of the game of nine ball that is catching on with both amateur and professional players. It is liked by tournament promoters because it is a fast game to play. It is a response to the perceived public boredom of the slow play and safety play used in many of the pocket billiard games. It is hoped that this game will help the sport gain additional TV coverage and increase the purses for televised tournaments.

The following rules modify the standard Nine Ball rules given on the preceding pages. The definitions provided at the end of the preceding nine ball rules still apply.

Initial break

Coin flip for break.

Subsequent breaks

Winner of game breaks

Legal break.

Cue ball (base of cue ball) must be within headstring. Breaker must strike "one ball" first then drive four (4) or more object balls to a rail. Penalty: rerack with incoming player getting the break.

Safety Breaks

Not allowed.

Scratch on break:

Cue ball in hand anywhere on the table.

Push out

Push out after break only.

Spotting balls

No balls spot, except nine ball.

Three foul rule

Three fouls in a row by the same player is a loss of the game; incoming player must warn opponent after second foul.

Jump shots

Legal jump shots only. No scoop shots.

Touching a ball

In an attempt to go around, masse, or jump over and object, if that ball moves as a result of hand, clothing, or cue stick follow through, it will be considered to be a foul.

If any attempt to shoot results in two (2) or more object balls moving as a result of using a bridge, hand clothing, or cue stick follow through, it will be considered to be a cue ball foul.

If any object balls are moved, opposing player reserves the right to place ball(s) in original position or leave lie.

Balls off the table

Anytime an object ball is driven off the table (ball does not spot), it is considered a table foul (but not part of the three foul rule). This table foul gives the incoming player two options: a) take the table as is; b) make the opponent continue as is.

DUTIES OF THE REFEREE

The referee will maintain order and enforce these rules. He is the final judge in all matters of fact. His duties include but are not limited to the following.

Before the Match

Before the match, the referee will clean the table and balls if necessary. He will ensure that chalk and mechanical bridges are available. He will mark the head string and long string with a pencil, if they are not already marked.

Racking

The referee will rack the balls as tightly as possible, which means each ball should be touching its neighbors. Tapping a ball into place is not recommended; it is preferable to through to brush the area of the rack to even out the cloth.

Calling Fouls

The referee will call fouls as soon as they occur and will inform the incoming player that he has ball in hand.

Clearing Pockets

On tables that do not have ball return systems, the referee will remove pocketed object balls from full or nearly full pockets. It is the player's responsibility to see that this duty is performed; he has no recourse if a ball rebounds from a full pocket.

Cleaning Balls

During a game a player may ask the referee to clean one or more balls. The referee will clean any visibly soiled ball.

Soliciting Information

If the referee does not have a clear view of a possible foul, he may ask spectators for assistance in determining what occurred. The referee will then weigh all evidence as he sees fit.

Warnings Which are Mandatory

The referee must warn a player who is about to commit a serious foul, otherwise any foul is considered to be a standard foul (except as specially noted). The referee must warn a player who has had two consecutive fouls, otherwise the player is considered to have had only one foul prior to the shot. The referee must warn a player when an object ball is touching the rail, otherwise any contact on that ball is considered to have driven it to that rail. The referee should issue warnings as soon as the corresponding situation arises. A warning given just as a shot starts is not considered sufficient; the player must be given enough time to react.

Restoring a Position

When it becomes necessary, the referee will restore disturbed balls to their original position to the best of his ability. The referee may ask for information for this purposes if he is not sure of the original position.

If the balls were disturbed by a player, the other player has the option of preventing the restoration. In this case, the referee should clearly indicate where the balls will be moved to if they are restored, and only restore the balls if requested to do so.

Advice and Rules Clarification

The referee must not give advice to the players on points of play except to clarify the rules. When asked for such clarification, the referee will explain the applicable rules to the best of his ability, but any misstatement by the referee will not protect a player from enforcement of the actual rules. When asked, the referee must tell a player how many consecutive fouls have been committed, what the score is, whether the cue ball is touching an object ball, what the restored position would be, etc.

Suspending Play

The referee has the authority to suspend play during protests by players and whenever he feels that conditions are unsuitable for play to continue. If a spectator is interfering with the game, play may be suspended until that spectator is removed from the area.

PLAYING WITHOUT A REFEREE

When a referee is not available, the player who is not shooting will assume the duties of the referee.

Third Opinion

When a shot comes up that seems likely to lead to controversy, a third person should be temporarily enlisted to provide a third opinion.

Resolving Disputes

Any dispute between the two players will be resolved by the tournament director or his appointed substitute.

Selecting a cue

For the individual just being introduced to the games of billiards, the purchase of a personal cue can seem to be an exercise in frustration. So many cue makers. So many grades and variations in the types of cues available. The variation in cost alone can create an information overload. What is the difference between a $20.00 cue available at the local discount store and the cues for $50.00 and more at your local billiard store? One very important difference is that your local billiard store knows cue sticks, how they are made, how to repair them, and how to help you select one that will fit the billiard games you will play with it.

As an example, the cue stick usually used in three rail (cushion) billiards has an eleven millimeter tip and is longer than the cues used for the games of eight ball and nine ball played on pool tables. A billiard cues, like a snooker cue, is generally a one piece cues The personal cue used for the games played on a pool table is generally a two piece cues

A good personal two piece pool cue will typically retail between $50.00 and $200.00, although the price can go as high as several thousand dollars for a one of a kind custom cue made by a known cue maker with expensive inlay materials (gem stones and precious metals) used on the butt of the cue.

The two piece cue is generally selected over the one piece cue for ease of portability. (Although the ownership and use of a two piece pool cue and it's cost undoubtedly have some bearing on the status of the individual within the local pool playing community.) With the resurgence of the game's popularity both pool tournaments and pool leagues (much like bowling leagues) are becoming popular in all kinds of places. (Billiard parlors, bars, and senior centers, to name a few.)

Winning pool players believe they play better and are more consistent when they always use the same cue stick. (Although you will find many money players (also known as hustlers) who will play and beat the best players in a local pool room using cue sticks from the wall racks. But from personal experience, the individual who wants to improve his or her pool game will do well to purchase and use a personal cue.

From experience, the best approach to buying a first cue is to buy a low cost quality cue from a known cue maker.

The specifications for a typical pool cue look like this:

Length	57 inches
Tip	Leather glue on
Tip diameter:	13 millimeter
Shaft	Maple
Weight	20 Ounces
Ferrule	1 inch fiber
Joint	Stainless steel to stainless steel
Butt	4 points wrapped with Irish Linen

The variations that can be made within this list are many. One cue maker has standardized on a fifty-eight inch length for its cues. Almost any pool cue can be purchased in different weights starting at eighteen ounces and going up in one ounce increments. (The more expensive cues can be obtained in 1/2 ounce increments.) Tip diameters can vary from twelve millimeters to fourteen millimeters. Ferrules can be plastic, ivory, and brass. Tips can be screw in or glue on. The joint can be wood to wood. The butt can be plain wood without any wrap or it can be a real work of art with fancy custom one of a kind inlay work. All these factors will affect the cost of a pool cue.

The grade of maple used on the cue shaft is one factor that will affect the price of your cue. Generally the tighter the grain in the shaft, the less likely the shaft will warp. But with a tighter grain shaft, the cue will tend to cost more.

The longer the ferrule the more a cue tends to cost. Then there are the ferrule materials. Ivory ferrules cost significantly more than implex (plastic) or fiber. Moreover, ivory ferrules are easier damaged with changes of temperature. You will also find the lower priced cues will tend to use implex ferrules.

The selection of the ferrule material also tends to dictate the materials used in other places on the cue. For example, a plastic ferrule tends to dictate plastic rings at the joint and the butt plate. Ivory tends to dictate ivory. The only exception is the cue with a fiber ferrule. Any joint or butt decorations on cues with fiber ferrules tend to be plastic.

On less expensive cues you can also find one piece slip on plastic ferrules and tips. You can also find screw on tips on lower priced cues. Then there is the ramin wood cue. This wood is softer with wider grain than hard maple. Therefore it tends to warp and become unstable in the first months of service. Although if the cue makes it through the first eighteen to twenty-four months it tends to hold up fairly well.

Other problems surface from time to time with the joints. Metal joints of dissimilar materials (brass to stainless steel or aluminum) tend to freeze together if the cue is left assembled for more than the short period of play.

Another problem that occurs with any cue made of wood is it will tend to warp if assembled and left leaning against a wall or table. It will also be subject to warpage if it is exposed to high humidity and extremes of hot and cold.

An aluminum cue may seem like a good idea but once the shaft is dented or the paint scratched it is permanent. A dent or ding in a wood cue can generally be repaired.

Other materials being used to make cues are graphite and fiberglass. All these exotic materials suffer from the same problems as an aluminum cue. Each can also have its own special problems that few cue makers and service centers can handle. These problems generally become apparent when re-tipping the cue or attempting to replace a broken or cracked ferrule. Sanding, trimming, and shaping a new tip can also cause problems.

Once you start shopping for a cue you will probably find cues in as many as five pieces with adjustable weights in the butt. The more pieces there are in your cue the weaker it is and the more likely it will break in normal play.

You also will find the butts of many two piece cues are wrapped with various materials (vinyl, cork, leather and polished linen are common materials). The more expensive cues tend to be wrapped with Irish linen.

While a wrapped butt looks nice it adds to the upkeep and maintenance cost. The wrap is supposed to absorb sweat created from the pressure of play. However, if you cannot control the effect of pressure during competitive play you should consider wearing gloves.

In choosing a cue, inspect the ferrule, shaft, joint, and butt for smoothness of fit and defects in the wood, fiber, metal, or wrap materials. A cue shaft with a tight wood grain is considered better than a shaft with a wide grain. Joints are especially subject to imperfections of smoothness and fit.

To check the shaft for straightness roll it on a flat surface (table, display case, etc.) and watch the space between the shaft and table surface. This space should not fluctuate at all if the shaft is straight. Now assemble the shaft and butt and repeat the process. If the space between the cue and surface now vary, the joint is out of alignment.

Cues made by established manufactures and cue makers are more likely to stay straight because the shafts are cured longer before being machined to their final dimensions.

Try many cues if necessary. Even if a billiard store lets you stroke balls with the cue, they will seldom allow you to rough the tip and chalk it up. Take this into account when testing a cue.

Feel the weight of the cue as you stroke. **The Science of Pocket Billiards** recommends that the first cue should weigh twenty ounces and be replaced with a lighter or heavier cue after you have played for a while.

The weight of the replacement cue depends on your accuracy verses your ability to play position. (The author of **The Science of Pocket Billiards** book believes heavier cues tend to make a player more accurate but do not allow for good position play.)

Feel the shaft diameter and taper as the cue runs through a closed bridge. Test the balance point and whether it feels good to you.

The only rule in purchasing a cue is to find one that you can afford and "feels" right. You will play better pool with a cue that "fits" you. How much you pay will depend on whether you select a one of a kind custom cue made by a well-known cue maker or select a low end production model pumped out by the hundreds by a known cue manufacturer. Both produce winning cues for the serious player.

To help you with your purchase, a list of North American cue makers is included as an appendix.

Things to consider when buying a cue

Tips:

>If you have a soft tip on your cue you will need to stroke the cue firmer to get the desired speed.
>
>A soft tip has a more surface contact with the cue ball. This allows for more english, draw, and follow to be applied to the cue ball.
>
>The playing characteristics of a soft tip have a shorter life than the playing characteristics of a hard tip.
>
>Softer tips hold chalk better than hard tips.
>
>The larger the tip diameter the larger the contact area. With the larger contact area it is easier to apply english to the cue ball.

Tip shape:

A tip with the same curvature as a nickel tends to maintain it's shape longer.

A tip with the same radius as a dime tends to cause fewer miscues.

Shaft:

The less obvious the grain is in a shaft the better the shaft.

The thicker the shaft the further forward the balance point is on the assembled cue.

European cue makers tend to make shafts that are the same diameter for eighteen to twenty inches. American cue makers tend to taper their shafts from the tip to the joint.

Butt:

A wrapped butt is useful only if your hands sweat. The popular nylon and linen wraps used on cue butts are used because they look attractive and are consistent in their feel and play.

Butt diameters vary. Some lighter cues use softer wood in the butt to reduce the weight of the cue. This also tends to make the cue less expensive.

To clean your cue shaft:

Use cigarette light fluid and old T- shirt or cotton balls.

Use a chamois cloth.

Rub it with a dollar bill.

Sand it with 600 grit sand paper.

Nick and dents

Nicks and dents in a cue shaft can be removed by:

- Taping a cotton ball soaked in water over the dent overnight. The water causes the wood to swell. Any bumps can be sanded down using 600 grit sandpaper.

  Using a piece of soft cloth (a T-shirt) soaked in water and a hot iron to steam the dented area. This allows dents to be removed almost immediately.

DEFINITIONS FOR NINE BALL RULES

The following definitions apply to both of the previous sets of nine ball rules.

Shot, Inning, Game, Match

A shot begins at the instant the cue tip contacts the cue ball, and ends when all balls in play stop rolling and spinning. (See *Miscue*.)

A player's inning begins when it is legal for him to take a shot and ends at the end of a shot on which he misses, fouls or wins, or when he fouls between shots.

A game starts when the referee has finished racking the balls, and ends at the end of a legal shot that pockets the nine ball or when a player forfeits the game as the result of a foul.

A match starts when the players are ready to lag and ends when the deciding game ends.

Above the Head String

A ball is above the head string if its center is above the head string (toward the head end of the table). A ball is below the head string if its center is below the head string (toward the foot or rack end of the table).

Stopped

A ball resting on the brink of a pocket is considered to have stopped if it remains motionless for five seconds, as determined by the referee. If any player or spectator causes such a ball to fall in before the five second limit by bumping or otherwise moving the table, the ball will be replaced at the edge of the pocket and is not considered pocketed. The time begins when all other balls have stopped and the shot ends at the end of the five seconds.

Pocketed

A ball is considered pocketed when it comes to rest in a pocket or enters the ball return system of the table. A ball that hits the lining of the pocket or another ball already in the pocket and returns to the surface of the table or jumps off the table, is not considered pocketed. If a ball comes to rest at the brink of a pocket so that it is partly supported by another ball, it is considered to be pocketed if the removal of the supporting ball would cause the supported ball to tall into the pocket.

To a Rail

A ball is driven to a rail if it is not touching a rail, and then touches a rail. A ball that is touching a rail at the start of a shot and then is forced into the same rail is not considered to have been driven to a rail if it is driven off the table or touches the pocket back or facing.

Spotting Balls

All object balls that have been pocketed illegally or driven off the table are spotted by he referee after the shot is over. Object balls are spotted by placing them on the long string, on or below the foot spot if possible, and as close to the foot spot as possible. If several balls are to be spotted at the same time, they are spotted in numerical order.

In Hand

When the cue ball is in hand, the player may place the cue ball anywhere on the bed of the table, except in contact with an object ball. He may continue to adjust the position of the cue ball until he takes a shot. With ball in hand above the head string, (after a scratch on the break), the player may not place the cue ball below the head string.

Off the Table

An unpocketed ball is considered to be driven off the table if it comes to rest other than on the bed of the table. It is not a foul to drive an object ball of the table. It is spotted and play continues.

Miscue

A miscue occurs when the tip of the cue stick slides off the cue ball due to insufficient chalk or to a contact point too far from center. It is usually accompanied by a sharp sound and a departure of the cue ball from its expected line of travel.

Lag

Players lag by shooting at the same time from behind the head string to contact the foot rail and then have the cue ball come to rest as close as possible to the head rail. Object balls may be substituted if two cue balls are not available. A player loses the lag if his cue ball crosses the centerline of the table, does not contact the foot rail, is pocketed or driven off the table, or hits any object ball. Ties are replayed. The distance of the cue ball to the head rail is the shortest distance between the cue ball and any cloth-covered part of the rail (the cushion nose or the pocket facing).

Push Out

The player who shoots the shot immediately after a legal break may play a push out. On a push out, the cue ball is not required to contact any object ball nor any rail, so the rules for a *bad hit* and *no rail* are suspended, but all other foul rules still apply. The players must announce his intention of playing a push out before the shot, or the shot is considered to be a normal shot. Any ball pocketed on a push out does not count and is spotted. Following a legal push out, the incoming player is permitted to shoot from that position or to pass the shot back to the player who pushed out. A push out is not considered to be a foul as long as no rule (except a *bad hit* or *no rail*) is violated. An illegal push out is penalized according to the type of foul committed.

General Glossary

ACTION: Used to identify whether gambling is allowed.

ANGLE: The direction a ball must take to strike another ball or cushion to arrive at a desired point.

ARTIFICIAL HAND: See mechanical bridge.

ANGLE SHOT: See *cut shot*

BAD HIT: The cue ball struck the wrong ball first. A foul.

BALANCE POINT: The point in the length of a cue that would be the fulcrum for a level cue.

BALL IN HAND: See *cue ball in hand*.

BANK SHOT: A shot where the object ball is driven to one or more cushions before being pocketed. Contact with a cushion parallel to the path of the cue ball does not qualify as a bank shot, unless the object ball hits a a second cushion. (The jaws of a pocket do not constitute a second cushion.

BAR BOX: A coin operated table often used in bars, lounges, and taverns. These tables can be either 7' or 8' in length.

BAR TABLE: Any pool table shorter than eight feet in length. Any coin operated pool table.

BED OF THE TABLE: The flat cloth covered playing area exclusive of the cushions.

BLIND DRAW: A method used to insure totally random placement or pairing of contestants in a tournament.

BOTTLE: A shaped leather or plastic bottle generally used to hold numbered peas or pills.

BREAK: The first shot of a game.

BRIDGE: The position of the hand that guides the shaft end of the cue during a cue stroke.

BUTT: The larger end of the cue. On a two piece cue the butt extends to the joint.

BYE: A method used for starting competition when there are not enough competitors to fill all the slots for the start of the competition. A competitor who receives a bye does not play until the next round of competition. A bye is used almost exclusively in the starting round of a competition and never deeper than the second round.

BUY BACK: A player who has lost the initial competition is allowed to re-enter a tournament at a bye position.

CALCUTTA: An auction of players before a tournament, with the auction proceeds used as prize money for bidders.

CALL SHOT: The player shooting must designate, before each shoot, both the number on the ball, and the pocket where the ball will be played.

CALLED BALL: The ball the player has selected for play.

CALLED POCKET: The pocket a player has selected for a called ball.

CAROM: The deflection of one ball after contact with another ball.

CHALK: A dry gritty substance, usually formed in a cube, that is applied to a cue tip to help prevent a miscue.

CENTER SPOT: Exact center of the table on both the long and short ways of the table.

CLOSED BRIDGE: Enclosing the shaft end of the cue for better control during a cue stroke.

COMBINATION: A shot in which the cue ball strikes one object ball that then strikes another object ball that is pocketed.

CONTACT POINT: The precise point of contact between two balls.

CORNER HOOK: To place the cue ball in the jaws of a pocket in such a position that an object ball cannot be contacted by shooting at it in a straight line.

COUNT: A successful shot - to score.

CRAZY BALL: A ball that does not roll true. A ball that is weighted in such a way that its center is offset.

CRIPPLE: An object ball that can be easily pocketed.

CROSS TABLE: To go from one side of the table to the other.

CRUTCH: The mechanical bridge.

CUE: The instrument used by a player to strike a cue ball.

CUE BALL: The white ball used to strike object balls. The white ball propelled by the cue stick.

CUE BALL IN HAND: A playing rule which allows the cue ball, after a foul, to be put into play any where on the playing surface.

CUE TIP: That part of the cue that is designed to come in contact with the cue ball. 1) The smallest end of the cue. 2) A piece of treated leather or other material glued to the end of the cue.

CUSHION: The cloth covered angled rubber which covers the inside of the rails. The outer limits of the playing surface.

CUSTOM CUE: A cue that has been made for a specific purpose or player. The butt of a custom cue is frequently inlaid with precious metals, precious and semi-precious gem stones.

CUT SHOT: A shot where the cue ball must strike the object ball off center to drive the object towards its desired destination.

DEAD BALL: A ball that is out of play.

DEAD BALL SHOT: A shot in which the cue ball is made to stop at the point of impact with the object ball. Also referred to as a *kill shot or stop shot*.

DEAD BANK SHOT: A shot where the object ball and the cue a ball are lined up so the object ball can be played off the rail without any adjustments to the angle of impact or reflection.

DEAD STROKE: A state of extreme concentration in which a player seldom makes a mistake.

DIAMONDS: The three marks between each pocket on the table rails.

DOUBLE ELIMINATION: A tournament in which each participant must lose two matches before being eliminated.

DOUBLE HIT: When the cue ball, after being struck, rebounds of the object ball and back to the cue tip a second time. A stroke where the cue tip touches the cue ball twice. The second stroke usually occurs after the cue ball is moving. A foul.

DOUBLE ROUND ROBIN: A tournament where each player plays all of the other entrants twice.

DRAW: 1) The pairing of competitors for a match by random selection; 2) To use reverse spin on the cue ball.

DRAW SHOT: The use of reverse spin, also referred to as reverse english, on a cue ball.

DROP POCKETS: A table that has been altered so the balls drop into the pockets when they would not normally drop into the pockets on an unaltered table.

DUCK: An object ball that is easy to make. Frequently an object ball that is sitting in from of a pocket or in the jaws of the pocket.

EIGHT BALL: A pocket billiard game in which the eight ball is the last ball pocketed by the winning competitor.

ENGLISH Rotational spin of the ball. Generally used in connection with striking the cue ball off center, but can be created when two object balls collide or an object ball rebounds off the cushion.

FERRULE: A fiber piece of the cue stick, varying in length from 1/4" to 1 1/4" just below the cue tip. It is usually ivory in color, but can be of colored material.

FOLLOW: Where the cue ball follows the object ball after the object ball has been struck. 2) A type of english created by striking the cue ball slightly above center. See top spin.

FOLLOW SHOT: A shot where the cue ball follows the object ball.

FOLLOW THROUGH: The continued forward motion of the cue tip after contact with cue ball has been made.

FOOT OF THE TABLE: The end of the table where the balls are racked.

FOOT SPOT: The spot on the center string of the table where the balls are placed when they are spotted.

FORCE DRAW: Occurs when the cue ball is struck below center. After striking the object ball and after hesitating or stopping the ball is drawn back towards its starting position.

FORCE FOLLOW: Same as follow only with a harder stroke.

FOUL: An infraction of the game rules. This can be something as subtle as a loose shirt touching a ball on the table to a double hit on the cue ball.

FOUL STROKE: An illegal stroke on a shot according to the rules of the game being played.

FROZEN: A ball in contact with another surface. i.e. Frozen to the fail, frozen to another ball, etc.

FULL BALL: To strike an object ball in such a manner that it travels in the same direction as the ball which hit it.

GAME: A single contest between two competitors. Any competition using specific rules.

GENTLEMAN'S CALL SHOT: Where obvious shots are not called, but all banks, combinations, pockets, etc. are called.

GRANNY: Another name for a mechanical bridge.

GULLY TABLE: A table in which the balls roll to a center point at the foot of the table. Commonly used on coin operated tables but also available on many non-coin tables.

HEAD OF THE TABLE: The end of the table with the manufacturers name plate. Also the end from which the balls are "broken." Also the kitchen.

HEAD SPOT: The center spot on the table even with the second diamond from the head of the table.

HEAD STRING: A "line" on the head end of the table that goes from the center of the second diamond on one side of the table to the other, passing through the head spot. On some tables this line may be drawn on the felt in ink. On other tables it is an imaginary line.

HIGH RUN: The maximum number of balls pocketed by a player in a single turn at the table.

HOLD: See stop.

HOOK: To place the cue ball behind an opponent's ball so the next object ball cannot be hit by shooting the cue ball directly at it.

HOUSE: A place where pool and billiards is played. An acronym for a pool hall or billiard parlor.

HOUSE RULES: Any modifications made to the standard rules of play by local players or a location where a competition occurs.

HUG THE RAIL: To cause a ball to roll while touching the cushion.

HUSTLE: To play below your highest skill level to entice a more inexperienced player into a money game.

HUSTLER: A player who hustles. Also someone to avoid.

INNING: A turn at the table. A player may remain at the table as long as they are pocketing balls or scoring points.

JAW: The edge of the cushion that extends into the pocket.

JAWED BALL: A ball that does not drop into the pocket but bounces back and forth against the edges or jaws of the pocket.

JAWS OF THE POCKET: The two edges on either side of the pocket.

JOINT PROTECTOR: A nut and bold that are used to protect the joint of a two piece cue when it is disassembled.

JOINT: The assembly point(s) of a multiple piece cue.

JUICE: See English.

JUMP BALL: Refers to a ball that has left the surface of the table. Also a ball stroked in such a manner to jump over another ball.

JUMP SHOT: A shot in which the cue ball and/or object ball is made to leave the surface/bed of the table. See masse.

KEY BALL: In continuous pool the 14th ball of the rack. It is important in obtaining position for the first or break shot of the rerack of balls.

KICK SHOT: A shot where the cue ball banks off of a cushion before making contact with the object ball.

KILL SHOT: Same as a dead ball shot or stop shot.

KISS: Contact between two balls.

KISS SHOT: A shot in which a ball makes contact with more than one ball. A shot where either the cue ball or an object ball makes contact with another ball to pocket the second ball.

KITCHEN: The area of the table between the head string and the head cushion.

LAG: To position a ball at a specific place on the table.

LAG FOR BREAK: Procedure used to determine the starting player in a game or match. Each player shoots a cue ball from behind the head string to the foot cushion attempting to return the ball as closely as possible to the head cushion.

LAY OF THE TABLE: The over all positioning of balls after the break.

LEAVE: The position of the balls, particularly the cue ball, after a player's shot.

LEFT ENGLISH: When the cue ball is struck left of center creating a clockwise spin on the cue ball.

LONG: Usually refers to a ball that travels at a wider angle that normal. Caused by English or stroke.

LONG RAIL: The side rails of the table.

LONG STRING: Line (if drawn) that would run from the center of the foot rail to the foot spot where balls are spotted.

MASSE: A shot where the butt of the cue is elevated to an extreme angle (30 to 90 degrees) causing extreme downward spin on the cue ball.

MASSE SHOT: Shot where the masse stroke or position is used. This type of shot is used in jump shots.

MATCH: The specified (or agreed upon) number of games. One or more sets between individual players to decide the individual winner.

MECHANICAL BRIDGE: A device that provides a stable support for the cue. Artificial hand.

MISS: Failure to complete a shot with the expected results.

MISCUE: When the cue tip does not make full contact with the cue ball. Usually accompanied by a clicking sound and the cue ball not going where it was expected.

NINE BALL: A game in which the competitor who legally pockets the nine ball first wins the competition.

NIP: A short sharp stroke.

OBJECT BALL: Any ball in a players set that is not a cue ball.

OBJECT BALLS: All balls used in a billiards game that are not the cue ball.

OPEN BREAK: An opening shot that drives a minimum of four object balls out of the rack to the cushions. Required in some pocket games to be a legal break. A break where the balls in the rack are spread on the table. Generally there are no object balls touching.

OPEN BRIDGE: The shaft end of the cue in a "V" formed by two fingers. Hand configuration for the shaft end of the cue to rest on during a shot.

PEAS: Small plastic balls that are numbered 1 to 15. These are used in various games or in a blind selection to determine partners in a doubles game or match.

PILLS: See peas.

POSITION: The placement of the cue ball after each shot in relation to the next shot.

POWDER: Talc or any similar substance used to reduce friction between the cue shaft and the players hand/bridge.

PUSH: Shot where the cue ball is pushed rather than stroked. Generally illegal.

PUSH SHOT: A shot where the cue stick remains in contact with the cue ball longer that allowed for a legally stroked shot.

RACE: The predetermined number of games that must be won before the opponent to win a match or set of games.

RACE TO "X": A predetermined number "X" of individual game wins used to determine the winner of a set. The first player to win "X" games wins the set.

RACK: A frame in which the object balls are placed to shape them before the beginning of a game. The rack is usually a triangle or diamond shape depending on the game.

RAIL: The top surface of the table not covered by cloth (usually wood) to which the cushions are attached.

RAIL BRIDGE: Bridge that takes advantage of the rail. A hand position that is used when the cue ball is close to or frozen to a rail.

REVERSE ENGLISH: When the cue ball is struck below the center of the ball. This puts *draw* on the cue ball.
RIGHT ENGLISH: When the cue ball is struck to the right side of center.

ROTATION: A game where the lowest numbered object ball on the table is the first shot. i.e. when the one is one the table it must be pocketed before the two can be shot.

ROUND ROBIN: A series of games in which all players play each of the other players at least once.

RUN: The number of object balls made by a player before a miss occurs.

RUNNING ENGLISH: The side spin on the cue ball that causes it to rebound from the object ball or cushion with a sharp angle and more speed that an ball shot without English.

SAFETY: A defensive play used to position the cue ball to lessen an opponents chances of scoring.

SCRATCH: The pocketing of the cue ball on a shot.

SEED: To place the best players so they have the best opportunity to meet in the finals.

SEEDING: The ranking of players by their abilities and playing records or wins.

SET: Two or more consecutive games between the same opponents.

SET-UP To position one or more object balls in a series of plays to make a run on the table.

SEEDING: The predetermined pairing of players in tournament play.

SHAFT: The narrower end of the cue stick to which the cue tip is attached.

SHARK: A person who engages in sharking.

SHARKING: Any deliberate action used to distract the players shooting. i.e. standing in the line of sight and swinging the cue stick; talking loudly, etc.

SHORT: A path a ball takes when struck with narrower angles than normal with no english or side spin on the cue ball.

SHORT RACK: Any game where less than fifteen object balls are used.

SHORT RAIL: The head or foot rail.

SINGLE ELIMINATION: A tournament in which a single lose eliminates a player from competition.

SLOP POOL: When slop shots are allowed with no foul or loss of turn.

SLOP SHOT: When a player makes a ball of his set that was not the targeted ball. i.e. After the cue ball strikes the targeted ball it caroms into other balls and one of the balls of his set is pocketed.

SNEAKY PETE: A two piece cue, that when assembled looks like a single piece house cue.

SNOOKER: A pocket billiard game in which 15 red and 6 non red balls are used.

SNOOKERED: To have been blocked from a clear shot by an opponent. (Snooker: When the cue ball is blocked by a ball or balls that are not on or in play.)

SPLIT: See split shot.

SPLIT SHOT: Where two object balls are hit at the same time. Where determination of which was hit first is unable to be easily determined.

SPOT SHOT: A shot that is made from behind the head string to a ball on the foot spot.

SPOTTED BALL: Any ball that has been placed on the foot spot after a foul or illegal shot.

SPOTTING A BALL: A ball is spotted on the foot spot after it is illegally pocketed. Other balls are placed directly behind and frozen to the first ball.

STANCE: The position of the body during the act of shooting the ball.

STOP SHOT: A shot in which the cue ball come to a complete stop after striking the object ball.

STRING LINE: Any line that can be drawn from one diamond to a diamond directly opposite it. Also refers to the line that is drawn from the foot spot to the center diamond on the foot rail.

STROKE: The movement of the cue as the cue strikes the cue ball.

SUCCESSIVE FOULS: Fouls made be the same player on consecutive strokes.

TOP SPIN: When the cue ball is struck above center causing the cue ball to travel the same path as the object ball. See follow.

TWO PIECE CUE: A cue having a butt and a shaft that are screwed together for play.

TRIANGLE: A triangular device, of wood or plastic, in which the object balls are placed to form them into the shape prior to the start of the game. Also referred to as a rack.

TIME SHOT: A shot where the cue ball strikes one or more object balls and continues on to strike one of those balls to score.

THROW SHOT: 1) A cut shot that changes the anticipated path of a ball by applying english. 2) A combination shot of frozen or near frozen balls where the first ball is hit by the cue ball and is thrown into the second ball causing it to go a direction opposite the cue ball.

WEIGHT: The measure of an object, usually refers to the weight of the cue in ounces.

WEIGHT CHART: A list of handicap systems that can be used by players of unequal skill.

WEIGHTED PLAY: A system of play that is designed to make play between players of unequal skill level more even.

HUSTLERS Glossary

Hustlers are con artists. As con artists they can give very convincing performances. They also attempt to gain every possible advantage. One way of doing this is by agreeing to a system of handicapping that *appears* to favor the player of lessor skill. While giving this appearance the hustler really believes the handicap is in reality money in his bank roll.

NOTE: The terminology used by hustlers can be very regional. These definitions are west coast based. Also many gambling games are played as call shot.

WEIGHT: The use of giving points to the less skilled or weaker player in a game. i.e. Used by the hustler.

WEIGHT CHART A chart listing different points of items that are used.

The following definitions are always referring to the weaker player in a game. Used in descending order with the 1st break to players who are almost equal to the wild five and breaks to largest difference in skill. i.e. The person being hustled.

1st BREAK: The first break of the balls is given to the weaker player.

SAFE EIGHT: Draw game

LAST TWO: The last two balls on the table are free for the weaker player.

CALL EIGHT: If the eight ball can be made as a result of a legal shot and is called (the pocket where the ball will drop is identified) the game can be won. i.e. If the ball can be made on a kiss shot, a carom shot, etc.

WILD EIGHT: Same as Call Eight but the eight ball does not have to be called.

LAST THREE: Same as last two but uses three balls.

CALL SEVEN: Same as Call Eight but using the seven ball.

WILD SEVEN: Same as Wild Eight but using the seven ball.

LAST FOUR: Same as last three but uses four balls.

CALL SIX: Same as Call Eight but using the six ball.

WILD SIX: Same as Wild Eight but using the six ball.

LAST FIVE: Same as last four but uses five balls.

CALL FIVE: Same as Call Eight but using the five ball.

WILD FIVE: Same as Wild Eight but using the five ball.

WILD FIVE AND BREAKS: This would conceded to the player with the least skill by a very skilled hustler.

Cue Makers

Alabama
Enterprise
K O Cues & Repair
1014 1/2 Rucker Blvd #3
205/347-7121
Fax #: None
800 #: None

Alaska
Delta Junction
Bender Cues
4952 Artic Graling Ave HC60
907/895-5273
Fax #: None
800 #: None

Arizona
Scottsdale
Robinson Cues
8321 E Evans Rd #101
602/948-5437
Fax #: None
800 #: None

Arkansas
Batesville
Hoyt Custom Cues
190 Swafford Rd
501/793-3043
Fax #: None
800 #: None

California
Anaheim
Katie Kue/R C Designs
4036 Leaverton Ct
714/630-8330
Fax #: 714/630-9282
800 #: 800/458-7958

Bellflower
Romero Custom Cues
17450 Bellflower Blvd
213/867-3580
Fax #: None
800 #: None

Canoga Park
Creative Inventions
7741 Alabama #11
818/883-5131
Fax #: 818/883-5817
800 #: None

Corte Madera
Fred's Custom Cue Shop
10 Tamalpais Dr
415/924-8844
Fax #: None
800 #: None

Duarte
Padget Cue Company
941 Crestfield Dr
818/357-1881
Fax #: None
800 #: None

Emeryville
Cousin's Custom Cues
PO Box 88008
510/528-1300
Fax #: None
800 #: None

Hawthorne
Allen's Custom Cues
14810 Kornblum Ave
213/675-4005
Fax #: None
800 #: None

La Crescenta
McWorter Custom Cues
3550 Santa Carlotta
818/352-0304
Fax #: None
800 #: None

North Hollywood
Ginacues
5424 Vineland Ave
818/509-0454
Fax #: 818/509-1231
800 #: None

Cue Makers

Schrager Cues
7255 Atoll Ave
818/764-0187
Fax #: 818/764-4073
800 #: None

Pleasant Hill
Chudy Custom Cues
1867 Lucille Ln
510/798-4369
Fax #: None
800 #: None

Riverside
Judd's Custom Cues
3191 Vallejo St
714/352-3776
Fax #: None
800 #: None

San Jose
Harry Sims Pro Shop
5160 Stevens Creek Blvd
408/984-7493
Fax #: None
800 #: None

Stanton
Tad's Custom Cue
8300 Cerritos Ave
714/995-1644
Fax #: None
800 #: None

Vallejo
Tweeter Cues
1815 Tennessee St
707/553-8969
Fax #: None
800 #: None

Colorado

Boulder
Moore Custom Cues Inc
5575 Arapahoe Ave
303/449-4076
Fax #: None
800 #: None

Colorado Springs
Kikel Custom Cues
1614 N Academy Blvd
719/596-7349
Fax #: None
800 #: None

Westminster
Showcase Billiards
12031 N Tejon St #202B
303/457-2501
Fax #: None
800 #: 800/783-7849

Connecticut

Marlborough
PFD Custom Cues
213 Flood Rd
203/295-8500
Fax #: None
800 #: None

Westport
Ralph Demattio
35 B Hiawatha La
203/222-1948
Fax #: None
800 #: None

Florida

Englewood
Cobra Cues
P O Box 732
813/475-5075
Fax #: 813/474-2322
800 #: 800/548-2837

Mizerack-Miller Custom Cues
P O Box 732
813/475-5057
Fax #: 813/474-2322
800 #: 800/548-2837

Fort Lauderdale
Picone Cues
630 SW Davie Blvd
305/767-9004
Fax #: None
800 #: 800/892-1417

Cue Makers

Navarre
Mace Cues
8132 Verano St
904/939-1454
Fax #: None
800 #: None

Orange Park
DP Custom Cues
2175 Kinsley Ave Ste 201
904/778-0479
Fax #: None
800 #: None

Tampa
Kierman Cues
1907 N Howard Ave
813/254-8795
Fax #: None
800 #: None

Robertson Custom Cues
1721 N Franklin St
813/229-2778
Fax #: None
800 #: None

Wayne Gunn Custom Cues
1811 Tampa St
813/222-0919
Fax #: None
800 #: None

Illinois

Chicago
Burton Spain Co
3724 W Division
312/235-2811
Fax #: None
800 #: None

Gumee
Dufferin Inc
4240 Grove Ave
708/244-4762
Fax #: 708/244-9752
800 #: None

Palatine
Madman Cue Co
P O Box 1542
708/358-0096
Fax #: None
800 #: None

Omega/DPK Cue Co
630 N Court St
708/705-1900
Fax #: None
800 #: None

Wright Cue Co
526 S Benton St
708/934-1022
Fax #: None
800 #: None

Peru
J & J Custom Pool Cues
822 Schuyler St
815/223-8774
Fax #: None
800 #: None

Wheeling
Schuler Cue (The)
1702 S Wolf Rd
708/520-7797
Fax #: None
800 #: None

Kansas

Witchita
Anderson Cue Manufacture
5130 W 9th
316/945-9833
Fax #: None
800 #: None

Kentucky

Bowling Green
Grimes Collectibles
10481 Cemetery Rd
502/842-9357
Fax #: None
800 #: None

Cue Makers

Nicholasville
J B Custom Cues
1615 Taylor Ridge Rd
606/887-5665
Fax #: None
800 #: None

Lousiana

Baton Rouge
Jensen Cues
9135 Cuyhanga Dr
504/924-4517
Fax #: None
800 #: None

Kenner
C's Custom Cues
4132 Loire Dr #d
504/466-1744
Fax #: None
800 #: None

Lake Charles
Gem Cues
P O Box 6364
318/474-3044
Fax #: None
800 #: None

Shreveport
Schick Custom Cues
4549 Old Mooringsport Rd
318/425-8565
Fax #: None
800 #: None

It's George
403 Lake St
800/343-6743
Fax #: None
800 #: None

Maryland

Baltimore
Lambros Cues
235 S Clinton St
410/327-5425
Fax #: None
800 #: None
Tim Scruggs' Custom Cues
3600 Georgetown Rd
410/247-1231
Fax #: 410/247-7459
800 #: None

College Park
Black Boar Cues
4908 Leigh Rd
301/277-3236
Fax #: 301/927-1847
800 #: None

Pasadena
Phillipi Custon Cues
182 11th St
301/437-2386
Fax #: None
800 #: None

Towson
Joss Cues Ltd
8749 Milander Ln
410/821-0064
Fax #: 410/821-8321
800 #: 800/245-5677

Massachusetts

Franklin
Pete Campbell Cues
19 Sunset Rd
508/238-6999
Fax #: None
800 #: None

Michigan

Ann Arbor
Dieckman Cues
PO Box 3191
313/761-3348
Fax #: None
800 #: None

Cue Makers

Oscoda
Norwood Products
3202 Railroad Ave
800/622-3221
Fax #: None
800 #: None

Mississippi
Brandon
Espiritu Custom Cues
2420 Hwy 18
601/825-7077
Fax #: None
800 #: None

Hattiesburg
Gilbert Cues/Magnum Amusement
422 Lemoyne Ave
601/264-8219
Fax #: None
800 #: None

Olive Branch
Meucci Originals Inc
7472 Old Hwy 78
601/895-4877
Fax #: 601/895-4634
800 #: None

Saucier
David Barber Custom Cues
21713 Saucier Lizana Rd
601/832-0102
Fax #: None
800 #: None

Missouri
Linn
Huebler Industries
P O Box 644
314/897-3692
Fax #: 314/897-4255
800 #: None

Montana
Missoula
Steel Stix
Box 4171
508/884-2222
Fax #: None
800 #: 800/735-3220

Nebraska
Lincoln
Elite Custom Cues
P O Box 4224
402/464-8401
Fax #: 402/466-3656
800 #: None

Neveda
Las Vegas
South West Cues
4608 Nolan Lane
702/870-9615
Fax #: 702/641-8488
800 #: None

New Jersey
Elizabeth
Palmer Billiard Manufacturing
307 Morris Ave
201/289-4778
Fax #: None
800 #: None

Gloucester City
Embassy Cue Co
56 Crescent Blvd
800/274-7665
Fax #: None
800 #: 800/274-7665

Mowhawk Cue Co
57 Crescent Blvd
609/742-7666
Fax #: 609/742-1239
800 #: None

Cue Makers

Glouscester City
Falcon Cue Co
56 Crescent Blvd
609/742-7667
Fax #: 609/742-1239
800 #: None

New Mexico
Alamogordo
Hunter Classics Custom Cues
172 Lahuz Gate Rd
505/437-1972
Fax #: None
800 #: None

New York
Lynbrook
Adam Custom Cues
25 Hutcheson Pl
516/593-5050
Fax #: 516/593-5896
800 #: 800/645-2162

New York
Mali Cues
257 Park Ave S
212/475-4960
Fax #: None
800 #: None

North Carolina
Ashboro
Stout Sticks
Rte 2 Box 102
919/629-6166
Fax #: None
800 #: None

Ohio
Cincinnati
Adamson Custom Cues
8809 Beechmont
513/528-2600
Fax #: None
800 #: None

Marysville
Tree Custom Cues
147 Buerger St
513/642-7670
Fax #: None
800 #: None

Mason
National Billiard Co
1111 Western Row Rd
513/870-0088
Fax #: None
800 #: None

Miamisburg
Hagencue
2107 Lionheart Dr
513/866-5875
Fax #: None
800 #: None

Oklahoma
Edmund
Guffey Custom Cues
2422 Cedar Oak
405/359-2047
Fax #: None
800 #: None

Mooreland
Prather's Custom Cue Parts
621 S Main St
405/994-2414
Fax #: 405/994-2700
800 #: None

Tulsa
Weinstock Cue Manufacturing
5626 S Columbia
918/744-1808
Fax #: None
800 #: None

Pennsylvania
Latrobe
Rainbow Cues
601 Main St
412/537-6827
Fax #: None
800 #: None

Cue Makers

Penndel
Szamboti Cues
320 Rumpf Ave
215/757-7280
Fax #: None
800 #: None

Pittsburg
Mottey Custom Cues
1628 Saw Mill Run Boulevard
412/881-9211
Fax #: None
800 #: None

Warren
Rauenzahn Cues
1608 Pennsylvania Ave E
814/723-8322
Fax #: None
800 #: None

South Carolina
Inman
Darrell's Custom Cues
1190 Campton
803/472-8028
Fax #: None
800 #: None

South Dakota
Sioux Falls
Keith Kustom Kues
1110 W 12th
605/335-3484
Fax #: None
800 #: None

Tennessee
Jackson
Bill Mc Daniel Custom Cues
586 Airway Boulevard
901/424-4455
Fax #: 901/424-4459
800 #: None

Johnson City
Cues By Fisher
429 W Maple St
800/481-6732
Fax #: None
800 #: 800/481-6732

Texas
Arlington
A Bear Custom Cues
PO Box 170 333
817/572-7944
Fax #: 817/478-4766
800 #: None

Bridge City
Jim's Custom Cues
705 Suddeth
409/735-2861
Fax #: None
800 #: None

Dallas
Libra Custom Cue
2833 Ripplewood Dr
214/324-3888
Fax #: None
800 #: None

Houston
Buss Custom Cues
15506 St Cloud
713/480-2893
Fax #: None
800 #: None

Pro Shop (The) - Bludworth
7614 Edna
713/641-1413
Fax #: 713/641-1212
800 #: None

Humble
Richard Black Custom Cues
2417 Bartletl
713/852-5025
Fax #: 713/852-7936
800 #: None

Washington
Bellingham
Brengamn & Brengman
3233 Sunset Way
206/758-7304
Fax #: 206/758-2300
800 #: 800/545-5912

Cue Makers

Kennewick
Benson Cue Co
516 E 1st
509/586-7277
Fax #: None
800 #: None

Seattle
Waldo Cue Company
7926 12th SW
206/529-1192
Fax #: None
800 #: None

Wisconsin
Bristol
Brunswick Billiards
8663 196th Ave
414/857-7489
Fax #: 414/857-7489
800 #: 800/537-7102

Eau Claire
Hawkins Cues
W3940 Box 50 Mitchell Rd
715/836-9196
Fax #: None
800 #: None

Green Bay
J P Custom Cues
4140 Velp Ave
414/437-7755
Fax #: 414/434-7757
800 #: None

Madison
Viking Cue Manufacturing
2710 Syene Rd
608/271-5155
Fax #: None
800 #: 800/397-0122

Menomonee Falls
McDermott
W146 N9560 Held Dr
414/251-4090
Fax #: 414/251-9290
800 #: 800/666-2283

Milwaukee
Schon Custom Cues
3812 W Burnham
414/383-9661
Fax #: None
800 #: None

Rice Lake
Schmelke Manufacturing
1879 28th Ave
715/234-6553
Fax #: 715/234-1026
800 #: None

Wisconsin Rapids
Jacoby Custom Cue
201 Ranger Rd
715/325-3696
Fax #: None
800 #: None

Travel Services

Airline Reservations

Air Canada
800/776-3000
514/879-7000
800/422-6232

Air France
800/237-2747
213/273-7833

Alitalia
800/223-5730

American Airlines
800/433-7300
817/967-1575

Braniff
800/272-6433

British Airways
800/247-9297

Continental
731/987-6500

Continental Airlines
800/525-0280
713/834-5000

Delta Airlines
800/323-2323
404/715-2600

Delta
404/765-2600

Eastern Airlines
800/327-8376

Gulf Air
800/223-1740

Japan Air
800/525-3663
212/310-1442

KLM Royal Dutch
800/777-5553
914/784-2000

Lufthansa
800/645-3880
212/745-0700

Mexicana Airlines
800/531-7921
310/646-9975

Midway Airlines
800/621-5700

Midwest Express
800/452-2022
414/747-4000

Northwest
612/726-2046

Northwest Airlines
800/225-2525
612/726-2111

Pan Am
800/327-5870
800/221-1111

Pan Am
305/873-3425

Quantas
800/227-4500

Sabina Belgiun World Airways
800/955-2000

Sas Scandinavian
800/221-2350

Travel Services

Southwest Airlines
800/531-5601
214/904-4000
800/442-1616

Swissair
800/221-4750

TWA
212/692-3311
800/221-2000

United Airlines
312/952-7843
800/241-6821

US Air
703/892-7020
703/418/7000
800/428-4322

Airlines
Airline Complaints
American
817/967-2000

Continental
731/987-6500

Delta Airlines
404/765-2600

Northwest
612/726-2046

Pan Am
305/873-3425

TWA
212/692-3311

United
312/952-7843

US Air
703/892-7020

Car Rentals
ABC Auto
800/524-2080

Advantage
800/292-5700

Agency Rent A Car
800/321-1972
800/221-8666

Alamo Rent A Car
800/327-9633
800/327-0400

American International Rent A Car
800/527-0202

Avis
800/331-1212

Budget Rent A Car Agency
800/527-0700

Dollar Rent A Car
800/800-4000

Europcar
800/223-1516

General Rent A Car
800/327-7607

Hertz Rent A Car
800/654-3131
800/522-3711

Holiday Payless
800/237-2804
800/729-5377

Travel Services

National Car Rental
800/328-4567
800/627-7777

Sears
800/527-0700

Thrifty Car Rental
800/367-2277

Tropical Rent A Car
800/367-5140

Credit Cards Loss or Theft

American Express
800/528-4800
800/521-9135

Diners Club/Carte Blanche
800/525-9341
800/521-9135

Discover Card
800/858-5588

Master Card International
800/826-2181

Visa
800/336-8472
800/277-6822
800/632-4730

Hotel & Motel Reservations

AMFAC Hotels
800/227-1117

Adam's Mark Hotels
800/231-5858

Aston Hotels & Restaurants
800/367-5124

B T H Corp
714/788-8380

Bahama Princess Resort
800/448-9385

Bahama Princess Resort
800/627-2760

Bally's Park Place Hotel Casino
800/225-5977
312/397-1300
609/340-2815

Best Western
800/528-1234
602/957-4200

Best Western International
800/528-1234

Beverly Wilshire
800/421-4354
800/282-4800

Canadian Pacific Hotels
800/828-7447

Clarion Hotels
800/228-5215

Colony Hotels & Resorts
800/777-1700
612/449-1900
612/449-1901

Comfort Inns
800/228-5150

Compri Hotels
800/426-6774
Continental Inn

Travel Services

800/432-9388
606/299-5281
609/293-5905

Country Hearth Inn
800/848-5767

Courtyards by Marriott
800/321-2211

Cunard Hotels And Resorts
800/222-0939
212/880-7500

Days Inns Of America
800/325-2525
800/325-3297
800/344-3636

Dillon Inns
800/253-7503

Disneyland Hotel
800/854-6165
818/562-3560

Doubletree Inc
800/528-0444

Downtowner
800/238-6111

Drury Inn
800/325-8300

Econo Lodges
800/424-6423

Econo Lodges of America
800/446-6900

Embassy Suite Hotels
800/362-2779
214/556-1133
214/556-8222

Exel Inns of America
800/356-8013

Fairfield Inn By Mariot
800/228-2800

Fairmont Hotels
800/527-4727

Four Seasons Hotels & Resorts
800/332-3442

Friendship Inns of America
800/453-4511

Galt House Hotels
800/626-1814
502/589-5200

Guest Quarters
800/424-2900

Hampton Inn
800/426-7866

Harley Hotels
800/321-2323

Helmsley Hotels
800/221-4982

Hilton Hotels
800/445-8667

Holiday Inns Inc
800/465-4329

Travel Services

Hospitality International
800/251-1962
Howard Johnsons's Motor Lodges
800/654-2000

Hyatt Hotels
800/228-9000
800/233-9005
800/233-1234

Hyatt Hotels Corp
800/233-1234

Inter-Continental Hotels
800/327-0200

Knights Inn
800/722-7220
800/866-6483
216/464-5055

LK Motels
800/282-5711

La Quinta Motor Inns Inc
800/531-5900

Las Vegas Sands International
800/367-2637

Lex Hotels
800/221-1074

Lexington Hotel Suites
800/453-9450

Lincoln Hotels
800/228-0808

Loews Hotels
800/223-0888

Madison Square Motel
800/821-4148
615/865-4203

Marriott Hotels
800/228-9290

Meany Tower Hotels
800/648-6440

Meridien Hotels
800/543-4300

Motel Six
800/437-7486
214/386-6161

New Otani Hotels
800/421-8795

Nikko Hotels Int'l
800/645-5687
212/765-4891
212/956-7430

Oasis Resorts
800/462-7472

Omni Hotels
800/843-6664

Outrigger Hotels Hawwaii
800/733-7777
808/922-5353

Plaza Fort Worth
800/223-1441
20037
202/452-9054

Plaza Inn Alburquerque
800/237-1307
818/905-8280

Plaza San Antonio
800/421-8811

Preferred Hotels
800/323-7500

Travel Services

Princess Hotels Int'l
800/223-1818
800/442-8418

Quality Inns
800/228-5151

Radisson Hotel Corp
800/333-3333

Radisson Hotels
800/228-9822
800/333-3333
612/540-5526

Ramada Inns
800/272-6332
800/228-2828
602/389-3800

Ramada Inns Inc
800/228-2828

Red Carpet Inn
800/327-0362

Red Lion Hotels & Inns
800/547-8010
206/696-0001

Red Lion-Thunderbird Motor Inns
800/547-8010

Red Roof Inns
800/843-7663

Regal 8 Inns
800/851-8888

Regent International Hotels
800/545-4000

Residence Inn by Marriott
800/331-3131

Ritz-Carlton
800/241-3333
404/237-5500

Rodeway Inns International
800/228-2000

Scottish Inns
800/251-1962

Sheraton Hotels & Motor Inns
800/325-3535

Sonesta Hotels
800/766-3782

Stouffer Hotels & Inns
800/468-3571

Super 8 Motels Inc
800/843-1991

Super Eight Motels
800/800-8000
800/843-1991
605/225-2272

Superior
800/322-8029

Susse Chalet Motor Lodges & Inns
800/258-1980

Tradeway Inns
800/631-0182

Travel Lodge
800/255-3050
800/261-3330

Trusthouse Forte Hotels
800/225-5843

Travel Services

Utell International
800/223-9868
800/387-1338
201/902-7800

Vagabond Inns Inc
800/522-1555

West Coast Hotels & Motor Inns
800/426-0670

Westin Hotels and Resorts
800/228-3000

Traveler's Checks Lost or Stolen

American Express
800/221-7282

Barclay's
800/221-2426

Cooks/Master Card
800/223-7373

Citi Corp
800/843-0777

Visa
800/227-6811
800/632-0520
800/227-6830

Travel Services

Index

A
adjustable weights, 70
airline complaints, 104
airline reservations, 103
aluminum cue, 69
auction variation, 32
auctioneer, 31
B
ball in hand, 36, 41, 46, 76
ball rack, 3
balls, 3
bar table, 8
billiard etiquette, 3
book making, 31
break, 35, 36, 41, 43, 53, 54, 61
bridge, 3
butt, 69, 72
byes, 27
C
Calcutta, 31
Calcutta Mechanics, 32
call shot, 51
car rentals, 104
chalk, 3, 4
coin operated table, 8, 11, 43
competition, 13
combination shots, 47
conceding, 15
concession, 58

credit card loss or theft, 105
cue, 67
cue ball, 25
cue specifications, 68
cue tip, 71
cue weight, 68
cushions, 26, 35
D
dent, 69
dents, 73
ding, 69
double elimination, 29
double hit, 48
dress code A, 5
dress code B, 5
dress Code C, 6
dress code enforcement, 6
Dynamo pool tables, 25
E
eight ball, 43
equipment abuses, 4
F
ferrule, 69
foot, 35
foul, 27, 37, 46, 54, 62, 64
frozen balls, 27
full pockets, 63
G
Gentlemen's call shot, 51
H
head spot, 35

Index

head string, 35, 44, 57, 75
hotel reservations, 105
house rules, 10
hustler, 3
hustling, 10
I
implex, 69
inning, 41, 75
ivory, 69
J
joint, 69
jump shots, 27, 38, 59, 62
K
kitchen, 10, 37
L
lag, 35, 53, 77
last pocket, 52
league play, 3, 13
legal shot, 35
logos, 7
lost or stolen travelers checks, 109
M
mechanical bridge, 4
miscue, 77
motel reservations, 105
N
nicks, 73
nine ball, 53

O
object ball, 25
one and fifteen, 52

open table, 45
P
pea bottles, 5
player auction, 31
player meeting, 15, 26
pockets, 25
push shot, 37
push, 61, 77
push shot, 27
R
rack, 4, 43, 53
rail, 76
referee, 14, 35, 63
ringer, 33
round robin, 28
rules, 64S
rules, 6, 10, 16
S
seeds, 28
scoop shot, 56, 62
scratches, 26, 44, 52
shaft, 70, 72
shaft diameter, 71
shaft taper, 71
shark, 18
sharking, 6, 10
social behavior, 5
single elimination, 28
spotting balls, 39, 62
spectator, 8, 18, 27, 49, 57
stroke, 26
T
table, 3

Index

table check, 26
talc, 3, 4
team competition, 4
Texas express, 61
time pay tables, 12
tip shape, 72
tournaments, 25
two piece cue, 67
U
unsanctioned competition, 6
unsportsmanlike conduct, 60
V
Valley pool tables, 25
W
wrap, 70

Index

Notes

Notes

Notes